For Alix

TABLE OF CONTENTS

INTRODUCTION

T HE WARM CARIBBEAN SUN PENETRATED MY eyelids as I floated in the gentle ocean surf. Here all my troubles, all my worries washed away with the soothing up and down motion of the calming waves. This is how life should always be, I thought. The ebb and flow of life, not harsh and pounding, but softly rocking. Somewhere, deep inside, I knew it was possible. I knew a peaceful center existed within me and within each and every soul on earth. Yet so few were able to find that place of calm centeredness—the inner knowing that all is well. The ultimate connection to All-That-Is. For these few moments, I'd found my elusive peace and savored every second.

Boarding the plane to return home to Atlanta, bidding goodbye to the beautiful white sandy beaches and Aruba's placating turquoise water, I reflected on the journey I'd been on for the last several months. Writing my life's story began as a personal project—a major step in healing. Originally, it was intended for my eyes only. Now I was contemplating releasing it to the public and sharing it with whomever would see it.

The decision to share my story with others was not an easy one. It would mean opening up in a way I never had before. Contrary to what the writing of this book suggests, I have always kept my thoughts, feelings, and issues closely guarded, so I struggled with this decision. Did I want to expose myself to the world? Would publishing it add to my healing? How would my family react? Why would anyone even be interested in reading about my life? More importantly, would anyone else benefit from it?

The answers became clearer as I wrestled with these questions. I'm in my sixties now, and, for the most part, I've been silent about the abuse I endured in the first ten years of my life. Aside from a select few, most people have no idea of what I experienced. But keeping my secrets has been like living with poison. It's been difficult to heal with venom in my system, constantly eating away at me. So many times I've thought the venom finally flushed out, only to have it reappear. My silence has kept the poison a prisoner. It is time to speak out and expel the toxin.

Why have I kept silent for so long? Fear. Family. Moreover, lack of family support. Fear of losing family. Shame. Vulnerability. Being ridiculed. Not being believed. Letting the world see the real me. But to fully heal, I have to move beyond these fears.

Countless people have been through similar situations, and mine is by far not the worst you'll hear. For abused individuals who come across this book, my wish is that they will find some hope or healing. Maybe just knowing that they are not alone will help. For others, perhaps they will become more aware of the pain and desperation so many children experience because of abuse. I hope it will increase awareness and understanding of the vast number of adults who are living with and trying to deal with the repercussions of abuse endured in childhood. For many it takes years or sometimes an entire lifetime to heal. Without a support system, some never heal.

The aftermath of abuse doesn't just go away on its own. From the time abuse happens it shapes and molds a person, often leaving that being emotionally and mentally frozen, unable to thaw out, to become the person they were meant to be. An abuse sufferer may feel like damaged goods, forever trapped by their past. But I believe that no matter how damaged they may be, as long as a person is alive, there is a little spark inside them waiting to be discovered. And if they can find that spark, they can grab hold of it and not only make it grow, but brightly glow for all the world to see. It takes determination and hard work, but most anyone can thaw out and make themselves pliable again, reshaping who they are, and ultimately becoming the person they were born to be.

Tranquility has certainly evaded me for most of my life. Finally, after so many years of darkness and struggle, I'm discovering my center, and, most importantly, how to stay in that center despite what is happening around me. It's been a long journey, one I am learning to appreciate. Only now can I see the sun does not need the darkness to shine. For years I held onto the darkness, letting it shape and control my life. I don't regret it. Without it I wouldn't have gathered the knowledge I have. I wouldn't be who I am today, and the more I get to know the real me, the more I value that person.

CHAPTER 1

A Child's Fantasy

AS A YOUNG CHILD, ON PRETTY spring or summer days I'd watch my mom hang out the laundry to dry on the clothing pole situated between the house and the garage. It wasn't a line stretched high above the ground from the porch to the far corner of the yard like at my grandparents' house, but a metal post cemented to the ground. Extensions at the top, where lines were strung in rows to form a square, twirled in the breeze. Following Mom out the side door and down the three cement steps to the yard, I'd take in the world around me as she set the basket of wet clothes on the ground, or the picnic table, and carefully hang each item out to dry.

I loved these days when I could watch the puffy white clouds float by on a deep blue sky and feel the grass thick and green between my toes. Closing my eyes, I'd turn my face toward the sun to feel its warmth as gentle breezes touched my cheeks and continued past me to flap through the clothes on the line.

Watching Mom go about her chore, a strong yearning would well up inside me. Longing to be one of those pieces of laundry, I fantasized I was as clean and fresh as the newly washed sheets. I wanted her to hang me up like the laundry she so carefully clipped to the line, freshly rinsed and spotlessly cleaned. And I hoped that when I was dry, she would take me down, immaculately clean, and fold me up and put me away with the other newly laundered items.

I've had this fantasy for as long as I can remember. In my late thirties, I began to understand what this strange desire was all about.

I was the fourth of eight children born to a middle-class, devout Catholic family. In the 1950s that meant birth control was not an option. Mom was only twenty-one and Dad twenty-three when they married. Ten months later they celebrated the birth of their first child who was greeted with love and excitement. The second child, another boy—born less than a year and a half later—was surely lovingly received as well. As the first girl, my parents must have been delighted when my older sister was born. But by the time I came along, two days before their fifth wedding anniversary, baby number four was undoubtedly beginning to push Mom and Dad into parental overwhelm.

Despite the quick arrival of so many children, my childhood seemed ideal in most ways. I grew up in a small community in upstate New York where most families knew one another, if not by friendship, than at least by name or sight. Quiet tree-lined streets, with names like Elm and Mulberry, were filled with comfortable Middle America homes where typical families dwelled, with dads going off to work and moms often staying home with the children. The town center, or what we called "uptown," was in walking distance of our home and provided my siblings and me with many hours of enjoyment. While the park in the center of the uptown area was a lovely green space with its trees and center fountain, my real love was visiting the shops around the park. My favorites were Gorton's where we could find bins full of wonderful treasures that could be purchased for a nickel or dime, the gift shop whose windows I daydreamed about, and maybe my very favorite, The College Inn, with it glass front display full of colorful and tempting penny candies.

Besides the shopping district, we could walk to the schools and their playgrounds which provided us with many an hour of enjoyment on summer days. We often rode our bikes to the community swimming pool in the summer or walked to the ice skating arena in the winter. There was plenty to do to keep ourselves busy and we were given the freedom to do it. It was a time when parents didn't think twice about letting their children roam freely around town. As long as we were home for dinner there were no worries. Mom took care of the children and made our house a home. Tending to the youngest ones, doing household chores, and getting dinner on the table promptly at five o'clock every evening kept her plenty busy. We were free to go where we liked, when we liked. We spent hours riding our bikes all over town—to school, the playground, the five and ten, the swimming pool, or a friend's house. No one worried about where we were, and it never occurred to us we could be in harm's way. It was a simpler time, a seemingly safer time.

CHAPTER 2

My Early Days

I'VE BEEN TOLD I WAS A "good" baby. This really meant that I was quiet, didn't cry a lot, and didn't demand much attention. Except for the crying part, these are attributes retained throughout my childhood. The best words to describe me as a child would be extremely shy, sensitive, quiet, and withdrawn.

Growing up, my earliest memory was of sibling number five arriving home from the hospital shortly after I turned four. It was a hot day in late summer when Dad pulled the car into the driveway and my playtime was interrupted for a brief moment as I took a peek at the bundle Mom held in her arms. Other than that, most of my childhood memories started when I began school.

Two weeks after my fifth birthday, Mom walked me to my classroom for my first day of kindergarten. We lived just inside the mile marker that would have allowed my siblings and me to ride the school bus, so we were "walkers." Our village had sidewalks the entire path to school and there were only a couple of small streets to cross before arriving there. I gained some independence early, as after that first day I walked to and from school on my own or with my older sister. Coming home from school was a time for dawdling and being free from teachers and parents. On fall days I'd kick through the leaves as I made my way home, stopping to rescue the prettiest ones to save for waxing. It snowed a lot from December through February or March and if I had bundled up properly I often stopped to play in the snow banks, make a snowball or two, or maybe some snow angels. On rainy spring days, prepared with raincoats and rainhats and rubber galoshes pulled over my shoes, I searched for the deepest puddles to jump in and slosh through.

Mrs. Bittleman was my kindergarten teacher. She lived in the last house on our dead-end street and the neighborhood kids called her "Mrs. Beetlebooper." In those days, reading and writing weren't taught until first grade, so our half-day kindergarten was mostly about learning to play with other kids and how to behave in a classroom setting. There was a lot of organized play time when we would color, paint, or play games.

On nice days we went outside. That was where I learned my first significant school behavior lesson. Several classes of kindergarteners and first graders were on the small playground reserved for those grades. All the children were having fun on the usual assortment of playground equipment—swings, slides, see-saws. On this particular day, the groundskeeper was on his riding mower and scheduled to cut the grass in our play area. The teachers lined all of us up and sat us on the sidewalk a safe distance from the mower. I sat opposite the triple see-saw with three balancing boards. The end of the middle board was up in the air, while the ends of the other two boards were down on the ground. For some reason this didn't seem right to me and I felt compelled to correct the situation. Jumping up, I ran over and hit the end of the board so all three were nicely lined up and matching. This felt much better until I found myself surrounded by three incredibly upset teachers. I must have given them a good scare, because they yanked me back to the group, scolded me for doing such a dangerous thing, and made me sit out the rest of recess. It wasn't a big deal. I was never in danger and the punishment was mild. But that day I learned the lesson of restraint and how to control my impulses.

Throughout my school years I did, from time to time, have the inner urge to correct something that didn't feel right to me. I'd have to contain my urge to get up in the middle of class and straighten the blinds or wipe the half-erased word on the blackboard. That early lesson taught me to squelch those feelings and restrain myself. But it wasn't just the little quirky things I used constraint on, it was most everything. Heeding the lesson of restraint, on top of my shyness, I rarely raised my hand in school or voluntarily participated in class. I didn't want to be singled out for doing or saying something wrong. It was better to just fade into the background.

Shyness often shut me down completely. It wasn't unusual for me to refuse to speak and I often wouldn't tell anyone what was wrong. One morning in kindergarten, I wore a coat which had recently been passed down to me. I hung it in the open community lockers and at the end of the day I looked for my coat, not remembering I hadn't worn my usual one. When I couldn't find it I was reduced to tears. I refused to answer the teacher when she tried to discern what was wrong. She was baffled by the situation as I remained sobbing and completely silent. It was as if someone or something inside took control of me and wouldn't let me speak. It wasn't that I wanted to keep quiet or didn't have anything to say, it just seemed the ability to open my mouth and speak up was beyond my control. I would often later regret not finding my voice.

At the age of six my family was holding steady at six children. I had two older brothers, an older sister, and two younger sisters. As most children do, we played and fooled around and rough-housed together. One evening things went a little too far. As my parents and grandparents chatted in the dining room, the six of us watched TV and played in our small den. An older brother, three years my senior, and I were playing a game in which I would jump on him, first from the floor, and then from the sofa. He told me to get on the back of the couch and jump. Being the obedient little sister, I did just that and landed on his arm. He let out a blood-curdling scream and the adults came running. His arm was badly broken. As my parents took him to the hospital, our grandfather gave us all a stern lecture about our rough-housing. It was the first time I'd ever heard my grandfather upset with any child, much less one of us.

The next day as I sat among the other children in my first grade classroom, the school nurse came in and recounted the incident (I suppose in an effort to prevent similar accidents). While she didn't identify which of the children in my family had been responsible for the broken arm, it didn't keep me from shamefully slinking down in my chair and hanging my head. My friend Maureen was sitting next to me and kept asking if it was me. I denied it, but I knew I'd already been named as the culprit. My mom was good friends with her mom and, as I would find out later, Maureen often heard about the happenings in my family before I did. I once gave her the exciting news that my mom was going to have a baby, something I had learned just that morning. I was crushed when she told me she already knew.

The guilt of the broken arm incident has stayed with me throughout my life. As a child, I let my brother hurt me by twisting my arm and such. To his credit, he never did more than make me suffer in the moment. In fact, I'm not sure he even realized he was hurting me.

My guilt over the pain and injury I had unintentionally inflicted on him kept me silent. It most likely wasn't this instance alone I have to blame for my sense of guilt, but guilt is an issue I have dealt with my entire adult life. Remorse and guilt are emotions that I seem to have internalized as a very young child and applied to many situations for which I had no responsibility. It wasn't until much later in life that I would begin to understand the shame and guilt and learn to let it go.

First grade was also when I learned to read and write using the Dick and Jane primers. Reading to myself was no problem but reading out loud was another matter. Unable to pronounce my s's, while the other children were reading "Stop Spot," I was reading "Top Pot." The hope I'd outgrow this speech impediment dwindled by second grade, so my teachers suggested I have speech therapy.

At first, speech therapy was kind of enjoyable. Being a quiet child in a large family, my voice was often overshadowed by my siblings. During speech lessons the therapist asked me lots of questions. She wanted to know about me, what I liked to do, how school was, my favorite subject, and so on. She listened carefully to what I had to say and asked more questions. I was delighted to have someone be so attentive to me, until one day I caught on. In truth, the therapist wasn't concerned with what I was saying, she merely wanted to hear how I was progressing with my pronunciation of s's. Once I figured that out, I clammed up and had very little to say to her.

The highlight of speech therapy was when my favorite TV dad, Danny Thomas from *Make Room for Daddy*, toured the children's hospital where my therapy sessions were held. Even though I was just seven, I could tell his appearance was a big deal. My session was interrupted and my therapist and I joined the crowd waiting to see him. He came by, talking to people and shaking hands, smiling and laughing. He seemed nice. As he stood right in front of me, I was tempted to reach out and touch him or at least say hello, but shyness once more got the better of me and I shrank back behind my therapist.

While the rest of the grade school classes were held at the new elementary school, second and third grade classes were taught at the old Marvin Street School. The Marvin Street School was a two-story red brick structure, originally built in the late 1800s as the town's elementary school. It has since been turned into apartments, but I rather liked the old building with its hardwood floors and how they expanded and contracted with the seasons. To a second grader, the wood floors seemed to rise up and down like ocean waves or small hills. My classroom was the first door on the right once you passed the stairs and turned the corner into the wide hallway. The first time I saw my teacher, Miss Callahan, I knew it would be a good year.

Miss Callahan did turn out to be my favorite teacher. She was the youngest teacher I ever had and I thought she was as beautiful as a movie star. Looking back at pictures of her, I may have been mistaken about the extent of her beauty, but she did have wonderful hair that fell around her shoulders in soft waves. I was more comfortable in her class than I'd ever been in school. She had an easy manner and didn't yell at the children or belittle us. I often stayed after school to help her with classroom chores like cleaning the blackboards or rearranging the desks.

The school administered a standardized test that year. Several years later, "straightening up" Mom's jewelry and junk drawer, I found a note Miss Callahan had sent home. The note was to inform my parents I had the highest IQ in my class. I was pretty impressed with this since my friend Maureen was in that class. She was extremely bright and would later go on to become a doctor. At the end of the school year Miss Callahan wrote a note on my report card: "When you give of your possessions you give little; when you give of yourself is when you truly give." Not understanding exactly what that meant, I thought she made it up especially for me, and figured she must have genuinely liked me to have written such a special note. I cherished it and have never forgotten those words.

My third grade classroom was located on the second floor of the Marvin Street School. There were a few classrooms on that level, more wood floors, and a large open area with a stage in the center. My teacher, Mrs. Lewis, was much older than Miss Callahan. She was tall and thin with neatly coiffed auburn hair. She almost always wore a pencil skirt, white blouse, and a sweater with the top button done up. When she wasn't wearing them, her glasses hung on a chain around her neck and rested on her sweater. By this time my shyness and withdrawal had reached an extreme level. My voice never rose above a whisper in class and my tears flowed often and with little cause.

I remember one project all the third grade classes were working on for a parent program. In our class we were instructed to select a bird, draw a picture of it, and do a report about the bird. I picked a road runner and worked hard on both my picture and report. Parents were invited to come to school during class hours. Each child was to go on stage, show their picture and give their report. When my turn came, I walked to the center of the stage, held up my picture, and stared out at the crowd of moms and dads sitting in the folding chairs. Overcome with stage fright, I stood there for a minute or two (although it seemed much longer), did not say a word, and walked off the stage. Another awkward moment of shyness.

Throughout my grade school years, lunch and recess were combined, giving walkers time to go home for lunch if they chose. I opted to walk the mile home where my mother was sure to have my usual lunch waiting for me—Campbell's Chicken Noodle Soup with Premium Saltines. It was a rare occasion that I packed my lunch box and ate at school. In fourth grade, back at the new elementary school, I did bring a lunch one day. My teacher was Mrs. Harrigan, an older woman who had been teaching for many years. I was one of her favorites (she taught my brother four years earlier and liked him which I suppose gave me an "in" with her). The day I ate lunch at school, Mrs. Harrigan chose me to head the line and lead the class from the cafeteria back to our classroom. Thrilled to be picked, I proudly led the class down the hall, making a sharp left turn into the adjoining hallway where our classroom was located. By the time we reached our room, Mrs. Harrigan, practically running in her high heels, caught up to me, mad as could be. She gave me a good scolding for not stopping and waiting for her "okay" before turning down our hallway. Standing there trying not to cry, her words piercing through me, she seemed to go on and on. I'd never seen her so mad. Being too timid to say anything myself, one of the girls in class spoke up for me. "Mrs. Harrigan," she said, "Shelley's never stayed for lunch before." The teacher was dumbfounded. She hadn't realized, apologized, explained the rule, and gave me a hug. Too late. The memory was already frozen.

CHAPTER 3

My Parents

MY PARENTS MET IN COLLEGE AND married. Before they even had a chance to adjust to married life, the babies started coming. They did the best they knew how and were good and caring parents in most ways. Dad was wrapped up in his role as the breadwinner. He grew up in a time when that was the part a man was supposed to play. He was good at it, intelligent, hardworking, and determined. Financially, he was a good provider.

Dad was a pharmacist, although filling prescriptions was not the focus of his career. His love was building his own pharmaceutical distribution company. When I was a child, it was a small company and he worked long hours and traveled a lot, promoting his products.

On weekends, he often went into the office and brought some of his children along to give Mom a little relief.

He moved out of his small brick office and warehouse building into a much more spacious facility when I was about six or seven. It was full of fun areas to play in, starting with the extraordinarily wide, steep stairs leading to his space on the second floor of the structure. On one side were several offices where my sisters and I would spread out in the various rooms and use the intercoms or phones to call each other. We pounded out words or nonsense on the typewriters, gave one another rides in the rolling chairs, and used each and every rubber stamp on the revolving stamp racks.

Just as much fun was playing in the warehouse. It was a large area with extremely high ceilings and rows and rows of tall shelves where he stored the various products he shipped. It was a perfect place for playing hide and seek and taking turns pushing each other around on the different utility carts and platform trucks used to fill orders. It was no problem to keep ourselves entertained while Dad went about his business.

Most of our interactions with Dad were as tag-alongs. He generally did the grocery shopping, mainly at a small grocery store named Carey's where they knew all their regular customers by name. If we were lucky enough to have a nickel in our pockets, we would ride the coin-operated palomino horse which sat in front of the store. Even better than the grocery store was when Dad went to Split-Rock where we got our huge glass jugs of bottled drinking water. When Dad returned the empties, we'd tag along. Split-Rock also bottled soda pop and this was one of the rare occasions when we were allowed to drink a carbonated beverage, so it was a big deal. We'd each pick out our favorite flavor (mine was orange), drink it right there, and then return the empty glass bottle to the used bottle rack.

Being part of a large family, it wasn't often we got dedicated attention from Dad. One special time that stands out in my mind is when he took my next younger sister and me to dinner at a "fancy" restaurant, The Golden Teapot. Eating out was a rare treat in and of itself, but to have Dad's exclusive attention was the best. With its linen tablecloths, china plates, and uniformed waitresses, it was the fanciest restaurant my sister or I had ever been to. In anticipation of our big night, we'd picked out matching white dresses with violet flowers and three purple straps on each shoulder. They were recent additions to our wardrobe, courtesy of the Boynton girls down the street who'd outgrown them. Other than making Dad guess where we'd gotten the dresses, I don't recall much about the dinner. But it was a unique enough experience to form a special memory—time alone with Dad. No competition for his attention, no one to call him away, no work issues to deal with, just his focus on two of his girls.

Mom left the discipline to Dad. His usual threat was "the belt." He did take me over his knees a few times and used his hand, but despite the threats, he never actually used the belt. The closest he came was one night when he and Mom were exasperated, having told all the kids countless times to settle down for the night. Dad threatened the belt if he had to come upstairs one more time. We tried our best to be quiet, but when the cat started biting my toes, my screams sent Dad running up the stairs with belt in hand. Only quick talking and pointing out the cat at the foot of the bed saved me. In general, I'm not sure he would have given any level of punishment if he weren't trying to appease Mom.

Dad worked hard and traveled a lot, leaving Mom at home alone with the kids a good bit of the time. She had her hands full and it often got the best of her. Mom had a lot of anger issues and her children were at the receiving end of them on a regular basis. The anger would build up inside of her until she couldn't hold it any longer. Then she exploded and unleashed it on her offspring. We never knew when it would erupt, but when it did it was loud and hateful. Although she directed it at her children, I think it was meant for the world in general.

She called us "no-good shitting bastards" and told us we were "nothing but goddamn H____'s (inserting our family name)." We often heard "I wish I'd died the day you were born." We were told we were nothing, no good, and rotten liars. The list goes on and on. Dad didn't fare any better than the kids and we heard how much she hated both him and his mother. She screamed these words at the top of her lungs as she held her hand flat across her mouth and between her teeth, as if she were biting it. I did my best to take cover in a closet or some distant corner until she finished. I wanted to disappear, to be anywhere but in that house. My fantasy was that I was adopted and my real parents would find me and take me away. Mom wasn't angry and shouting all the time, but for a sensitive child like me, these words screamed during her rages had a deep and lasting impact.

Although I never saw my friends' parents act this way, I assumed they were on good behavior when other people were around. I grew up thinking the rage, screaming, and accusations were normal until some of the neighborhood kids commented on her rants. With no air conditioning, the windows were always open in the summer and the whole neighborhood could hear her tirades.

But Mom wasn't a monster. She took her responsibilities seriously. We could count on supper being on the table every night, having clean clothes to wear, and as reasonably clean a house as possible with all of us youngsters running around. When she was relaxed, Mom could be fun to be around. She loved to sing, did a lot of baking, and every now and then enjoyed teaching us parlor games and playing them with us. We had family nights when we ate popcorn and watched home movies. She taught us to play card games and enjoyed recounting stories from her childhood.

Unfortunately, these times didn't erase the words slung at us in fits of rage. From an early age, I internalized and took her words to heart, often blaming myself for causing her rages. Maybe I should help more around the house, or try harder not to fight with my siblings... I felt an irrational guilt for erupting emotions that most likely began simmering inside my mother long before I was born.

Aside from a half-sister who was ten years older, Mom was the eldest child in her family. Her dad was controlling and strict and, while the family bonds were strong, there was not a lot of outward affection. The trend continued with her own family. Growing up I only remember being told I was loved when it was part of a punishment or explanation of why I couldn't do something. "We love you but . . ." Hugs were rare and good night kisses were blown from the doorway, if at all. As for Dad, his father died of TB when Dad was around ten or eleven years old, leaving him without a father figure to emulate. He followed Mom's pattern of affection.

Every child needs to know they are loved. My parents loved us but didn't know how to show it—at least not in the way I wanted to be shown. They did the best they knew how, but hugs, kisses, kindness, caring, attention, and the words "I love you" were all in too short supply.

CHAPTER 4

Life In Atlanta

WHEN I WAS FOURTEEN, DAD SOLD his pharmaceutical company and we moved to the suburbs of Atlanta. Here he served as vice-president of the similar, but larger company that had purchased his business. Before joining him in Atlanta, Mom entrusted Dad with picking out our new residence while she stayed at home in upstate New York with the children. He found a large five bedroom, three bathroom traditional style, two-story brick home up the street from an affluent Catholic church with a parochial elementary school. It was also within walking distance of the public high school my older sister and I would be attending. Although anxious about leaving behind our friends and family, we were excited when we saw pictures of this beautiful house, and it seemed ideal for a family that now included eight children. By this time my oldest brother was in college and my next brother stayed in New York with my grandparents to finish his senior year in high school. For the first time since I was a toddler, I had a bed to myself and was sharing a room with one sister instead of three. As new and beautiful as this house was, it never felt like "home." It was merely a nice house in which to live.

Knowing that leaving our life-long home would be traumatic for us, Mom and Dad promised we could buy a horse when we moved to Atlanta. They kept that promise and my sisters and I spent most of our free time after school and on weekends riding and taking care of Forio (named after the horse in Alfred Hitchcock's movie Marnie). We soon added a second horse named Star. For the most part, the horses kept us happy and out of trouble as we adjusted to our new home and schools.

Before the move to Atlanta, I was in my first semester of ninth grade at a Catholic high school. Since uniforms were required at that school, my clothing selection for my new school was limited and mostly of my own construction. Getting dressed for my first day at school after the move, I put on my best outfit—a brown herringbone skirt and jacket with a pretty, ruffled blouse. It was apparent from day one that I was out of place. The kids were rich and snobby and my homemade clothing definitely did not fit into the trendy, preppy looks most of the teenagers wore.

Managing to make friends with a couple of other outsiders, my style gradually changed, but not to the looks the popular girls were wearing. By my junior year I was trending toward the hippie clothing and lifestyle. But along with my hippie style clothing, drugs were also becoming a part of my life—at first mostly smoking weed, later turning to amphetamines, and eventually barbiturates. It started out slowly at first, just social use and wanting to fit in with my new friends. Perhaps the clothes and drugs were just normal teenage rebellion. Or maybe I was trying to soothe an inner storm that was brewing. Although at the time I didn't consciously recognize it, looking back now I can see there was a pain deep inside of me, a pain that could be lessened, or ignored, with the help of the drugs. But I was careful and hid my drug use from my parents. My older sister was more on the "wild" side and often in trouble with them, while I still appeared to be the "good girl." I wanted to keep that image.

Within two years of moving to Atlanta, we owned three horses and my mom was getting tired of driving us back and forth to the farm where we pastured them. We began the search for a new home with some land. After a long hunt, we found the perfect place in Crabapple—six acres with an almost new, one-year old, custom-built house with fenced pastures, a practice ring, and a recently constructed horse barn with plenty of room for all our horses, tack, and feed. As soon as we walked through the door of the house, we knew we'd found our new home. It just felt right. The house was only three bedrooms, but there were two large rooms, one finished and one unfinished, plus a bathroom in the daylight basement. The four girls were happy to claim this area as their own space.

My senior year began at a new school. Milton High School was a culture shock, to say the least, although today it has no resemblance to the rural area institution it was in the early '70s. I was in disbelief that I was attending a high school where the person sitting next to me might be married or have a baby at home and it was perfectly acceptable. But even with the different values, I was more comfortable with these kids than the snobby classmates I'd left behind. Managing to find some new friends and beginning to date much more, I stumbled through my last year of school. Drugs, (which by now included LSD, something my newest friends were experimenting with and another means of leaving reality behind), and sex were of more interest than my studies. I barely passed most of my classes, but somehow managed to graduate on schedule.

Unlike my brothers, the girls in our family hadn't been groomed to go to college. Maybe it was that my parents thought that as girls we didn't need a college education (although my mother was a college graduate) or perhaps they were in financial or emotional overwhelm with so many children. Either way, the four girls in the middle slid by without much notice as to their school work, grades, or taking of SAT tests. No one offered to take us on college visits as was done with the four boys in the family. The fact that my parents had not encouraged their daughters' higher education was a sore spot for me for many years. At the time, I took the attitude that if they didn't care, why should I? It took me a long time to let go of the resentment and take responsibility for my own decisions not to continue with school.

Still living with my parents, I worked at a couple of different jobs, first as a clerk at a greeting card shop in the mall, then a year in the billing department of the phone company. A year or so after graduating high school, I was anxious to be out on my own. My friend Pam felt the same way. Signing a one-year lease, Pam and I moved out of our respective parents' homes into a brand new two-bedroom apartment. During the year we shared an apartment, Pam introduced me to metaphysics. The concepts of reincarnation, spirits, psychics, and guided meditations were new and exciting ideas that made sense to me. I had discarded my Catholic upbringing by my mid-teens, so I welcomed this new way of thinking. Pam invited me to accompany her to one of her metaphysical classes. After my first guided meditation (a vision of myself growing larger and larger until I was holding the entire world in my hands) I was hooked. This and similar classes helped me expand my psyche and my awareness of life. I learned Transcendental Meditation, which was popular at the time, and I practiced it for quite a while. It had a calming, centering effect on me. My beliefs have changed and grown over the years, but the metaphysical concepts I learned that year became the basis of my current belief system.

I became disillusioned with the phone company and left my nine to five desk job to wait tables at an upscale restaurant for the lunch shift and a local pizza establishment in the evenings. By this time I'd cleaned up my act and had stopped most of the drug use. The year in the apartment was a great year of independence, however, as our lease neared its end I was beginning to realize that the jobs I worked were getting me nowhere, so I decided to give college a try.

I moved back into my parents' home and enrolled at the local junior college. Being interested in psychology, my hope was to someday get my PhD. However, my return to school was short-lived. I dropped out at the beginning of my second year after enrolling in a required English course that necessitated a good bit of creative writing. This had always been a problem for me and I soon found out creative writing was still an issue. It felt like torture to try to get a few words on paper. I was back in fourth grade again, wanting to hide under my desk if the teacher made any part of my paper an example. The trauma was too much. When I realized I could not get through this course I gave up college altogether.

At the time, I didn't know why I had such an issue with writing. I was making As in all my other classes, but this one turned my stomach inside out. Looking back now, it is clear to me that the walls I'd built to protect myself were also keeping me from achieving many of my goals. Letting anyone see inside me was just too painful. There were secrets that had to stay hidden, even from me.

Dad always had a fondness for retail, so when an opportunity opened up to buy out a plastercraft store that was closing down, he jumped at the chance. Painting figurines and other items from the closing store was a hobby several in the family had taken up. Reopening in a new location, my youngest sister and I ran the shop and enjoyed interacting with the customers and unleashing our creative sides by painting and applying various finishes to the statues and other whiteware pieces we sold at the shop. When the mall was remodeled a year later and our rent tripled, we closed the store. Still searching for something meaningful to do with my life, I tried my hand at real estate and worked at a couple of other jobs, but didn't find anything that suited me.

I was unemployed and searching for a direction in life, but with no clue as to what I wanted to do. By this time my family's situation had changed. Dad was never meant to work for anyone else; he liked to do things his way. He'd resigned his VP position and again began building his own pharmaceutical company. At first it was Dad and Mom working by themselves in the office, but as the company grew, Mom was desperate for help. So, being available, I went to work for them. Working in a small office and learning all the various aspects of the business—everything from accounting in the front office to pulling and shipping orders in the warehouse—proved to be good experience that would later be utilized in other jobs.

CHAPTER 5

Meeting Glenn

AS A TEENAGER, I DECIDED MY perfect age to get married would be twenty-five. No specific reason, it just seemed like the right age and that number always stuck with me. My twenty-fifth birthday came and went and there was no one special in sight. In fact, I was rarely dating, having decided a couple of years before that it was better not to date than to spend my time with guys that weren't what I was looking for, although I'm not sure I knew what that was. Still living at home, working for my parents, my life was stagnant. If I wanted anything to change, I needed to do something different.

I decided to give school another try and as September rolled around,

I registered for an evening class at a nearby community college. The first night of class I found a seat and made my acquaintance with a couple of people sitting nearby. I looked up right before class got underway and in walked a tall guy with a beard and a motorcycle helmet under his arm. As the weather was turning chilly, he wore a one-piece thermal motorcycle suit making him look a little like an abominable snowman. The moment I saw him my heart skipped a beat and I heard myself think "That's him! That's the man I'm going to marry." My rational mind took over quickly and with my second thought I asked myself, "What? Are you crazy?"

He sat in the row next to me, one seat behind. We kept our seats each week and he became part of our little group of four or five that would chat before class, although I rarely spoke to him directly. One night he asked for my phone number and on November 16th we went out on our first date. It was on that date that he told me he loved me and was going to marry me. Three weeks later we were officially engaged, and on February 16th, exactly three months after our first date, we were married. I was still twenty-five at the time.

Seeing Glenn for the first time and feeling my heart skip a beat was not due to a physical attraction. It was much stronger than that. It was a soul recognition.

When I met Glenn, I was still working for my mom and dad. That job worked out for a while, but working for family can be trying, and after a couple of years of being employed by my parents, the daily pressure was too much and I gave them my notice. We were living paycheck to paycheck and I wasn't sure what kind of job I would find. Glenn encouraged me and assured me my skills were good, helping to boost my confidence. He was right. With the experience gained, I had two respectable job offers within a week.

A year or so after we married, Glenn and I bought our first little house—a modest older remodeled home with two bedrooms and one bathroom. A couple years later our first child, a boy we named Adam, was born. I felt fortunate to be able to stay home with Adam, earning a little extra cash by taking care of a friend's baby a couple days a week. When the next baby came along not quite two years later—a girl named Alix—I could no longer financially afford to stay home. My younger sister had replaced me at Dad's pharmaceutical company when I left and now her first baby was due only four months after Alix was born. When she went on maternity leave I found myself working at the family business again.

By this time, Dad's company was located in his own larger facility he'd had built to meet the needs of his expanding enterprise. My older brothers had both joined him in running the business, so this time around I was surrounded by even more family, but it worked out okay. With the growing business there were also non-family employees, making for easier working conditions than my previous situation of working with just Mom and Dad in the office. There was plenty to do. The company was growing and I was taking on more and more responsibility, overseeing several others as office manager, and helping out managing the inventory and marketing and sales staff for a newly acquired manufacturing facility. Financially, Glenn and I were over the "just starting out" phase of trying to make ends meet. There wasn't a lot of excess money, but we were comfortable enough.

Our little family of four moved into a bigger house when Alix was eight months old. Glenn had received a job offer around the time Alix was born, but right from the beginning he was miserable in his new position. The next year Glenn left his management job to return to the service sector, working on set-ups and installations for office buildings. It was less money, but he was much happier. Money was tight again and I was feeling the pressure and working harder and harder to prove my worth at work. In some ways, I think I was trying to show that I was just as valuable to the company as my brothers who had college degrees. I worked long hours, often bringing work home to continue through the evening. But I was only a girl, and in my dad's eyes girls didn't make as much money as the guys.

CHAPTER 6

Getting Restless

OVER THE YEARS, WORK, MARRIAGE, AND family became the focus of my life. My interest in meditation and metaphysics took a backseat. In my late thirties, a restlessness began to stir within me. I felt a need to grow, to be more than I was, for my life to be more than it was. I began to meditate again, thus beginning a ride I couldn't have foreseen. During meditation, tiny, fleeting images appeared in my mind. What were they all about? What was my life all about? My interest in metaphysics was being rekindled. I needed to move beyond my ordinary everyday life. There had to be more to my existence.

The search for answers led me to a local New Age book store,

SunGlo. As I wandered around this charming shop with its comfortable atmosphere, Gloria, the owner, asked if there was anything special I was looking for. Having come in with only a desire to rekindle my connection to metaphysics, I started to answer no, but was surprised to hear the words "a book on dreams" coming out of my mouth. I'd been a vivid dreamer all my life, and the book she suggested, *The Mystical Magical Marvelous World of Dreams*, helped me make sense of them. Decoding dreams gave me insight into the path I was beginning to follow. In my early days of interpreting them, this one stands out:

> *I get into the front passenger seat of a car. A former co-worker, Chris, gets in the driver's seat. I look at some kind of book, trying to find somewhere to go, but not having much luck. Chris suggests we go to an area she calls "home" and says I should check the book for directions. Chris pulls out of the driveway without looking and turns right. She drives down the middle of the road and another car has to swerve. It's forced up a green grassy hill and then it returns to the road. As a result of Chris pulling out into the road, three cars crash. We are able to avoid the accident and continue down the road, a two-lane country road with many trees on either side. We quickly round a curve and lose sight of the accident. Before getting out of sight, I look back and see one red-haired man is out of his car and shaking his fist at us. I feel responsible (for the accident and upsetting others) and wonder if we should stop, but Chris keeps driving.*

Previously I'd found dreams to be entertaining, puzzling, amusing or sometimes frightening, but with the help of the book it became clear they were full of messages: Chris (who was especially spiritual) represented my Christ-self. Since she was in the driver's seat, I determined this represented me letting my higher self guide my life. Not having much luck finding someplace to go commented on my feelings of discontent with my current life's path. Chris's suggestion to go "home" was leading me to my source (God). Pulling out without looking was saying "Just do it!" Turning to the right and the country road indicated going in the right direction on my spiritual journey. The other vehicles signified people who would try to get in my way.

The overall message I received from the dream was that I was on the right spiritual path for me. Even if others tried to get in my way or were angry with me for taking this path, I should keep going and not look back.

We each must interpret our own dreams and find meaning in how they relate to our individual lives, but this book was a great place to begin grasping the significance of my dreams. It taught me how to keep a dream journal and instructed me in techniques to remember my dreams.

On my next visit to the book store, Gloria wisely told me to browse around and see what "called to me." She looked surprised at my pick (Abraham-Hicks first book *A New Beginning* I) but I felt strongly drawn to it. I went home and began to read it. In the early 90s, the idea that we create our own reality was unfamiliar to me and deeply upsetting. I was responsible for creating my life? It wasn't just happening to me? After the first chapter, I put the book down and didn't pick it up again for a year. When I finally decided to try it again, the timing was right. I could hardly put it down, absorbing the information, though not applying much of it yet or thoroughly understanding it.

Since reading their first book, the Abraham-Hicks material has been my most constant source of inspiration and guidance. I have read all their books and listened to countless CDs. Abraham teaches The Law of Attraction, helps us understand how we create our own reality, how to manifest our desires, and that the purpose of our lives is joy.

I wish I could say I quickly grasped the information they offered and immediately put it to use in my life, but that hasn't been the case. It has been a slow process of gradually absorbing the concepts and incorporating them into my life. Despite my resistance, they have been a tremendous help in my healing.

Visiting SunGlo and attending the psychic fairs Gloria held became a regular occurrence for me. I immediately felt at ease with a psychic named Angie. She posed a question to me: Where was all my anger coming from? Anger issue? I was oblivious to a lot of things in my life at that point, but when I contemplated her question, she was right. I'd been blaming my outbursts on my "time of the month." This always seemed to be when I'd go out of control. There was a madness inside of me which seemed to come out of nowhere. My house and my husband took the brunt of this fury. Slamming doors as hard as possible helped me to release a little of the anger. Screaming at my husband and blaming him for all my problems also relieved some of the rage. In the days leading up to my period, emotions and thoughts I didn't experience during the rest of the month exploded within me. I'd been blaming all these feelings on hormones and it never occurred to me to look for an underlying cause.

CHAPTER 7

The Frozen Children

MY ENTIRE LIFE I'VE FELT AS if I didn't belong. A sense of being different has always been with me. Why did I feel so unlike other people, so out of place? Feelings of loneliness and isolation often overtook me. I never quite fit in and I wanted to know why. Deep inside there was a strong desire to discover what made me tick. Why was I the way I was? Could I change? Would I ever feel comfortable with my existence? I needed answers to the questions and emotions stirring inside me.

Going to a traditional psychologist or psychiatrist didn't feel right. Gloria pointed me in the direction of Apollonia, a new age empath whom I began to see on a weekly basis. The first half of each session we talked. Up until this point I'd kept my walls up, effectively shutting everyone out. With Apollonia it was easy to let my guard down and be open. I felt safe and comfortable with her. For the first time, I had someone I could talk to about anything, and there was much more to talk about than I could have imagined.

After our talk, I'd lie on a vibration table (a relaxing waterbed that vibrates) while listening to tapes which utilized Acoustical Brain Research. This psychoacoustic technology, which had an affect on beta, alpha, and theta brain waves, sometimes contained comforting stories with subliminal messages, others incorporated music frequencies designed to stimulate those brain waves. These sessions were powerful for me. Inner forces were clamoring to get out, although prior to these sessions, I had no way to release them.

Apollonia gave me a set of tapes to listen to at home after our first session. She kind of shook her head, handed me another tape called "Transformation Now," and told me "I never give this tape out. It is very powerful, but my spirit guides are telling me to give it to you." Powerful was an understatement. Those tiny images that had come up in meditation were now surfacing as full-blown pictures and movies in my mind. Long-repressed memories were being unleashed.

I took every opportunity to work on myself between sessions. I would listen to the tapes when the kids visited their grandparents, their dad took them to soccer practice, or whenever I could find a few minutes for myself. The term "inner child" quickly took on a new meaning for me. As I lay on my bed and listened, images often appeared in my mind. Children began to emerge. Talking to the most prominent child that appeared, I learned her name was Shelli. For some time she would act as my guide, revealing other inner children when they were ready to surface and protecting those that weren't yet ready. Following are some journal entries from my work with Shelli:

3/12 (Early morning; Listening to Emotional Overwhelm Tape) Shelli joined me in listening to the tape. She is so alone and there is so much inside her. She let me take her hand and lead her outside. We stood together and watched the river flow. We sat down and I held her.

(Mid-morning; listening to Eliminating Self-Sabotage Tape) Shelli joined me again. We walked hand in hand through the forest. I held her close as a cocoon wrapped around us. It's as if she's my child now and I have to protect her. I cried hard after this tape. She wants so much to be loved.

(Mid-afternoon; Self-Esteem tape) Shelli slept. As I traveled (in my mind) I told her if she needed me, all she had to do was think of me. I felt peaceful, ready to rest.

(Evening; Transformation Now tape) Shelli led me down the basement stairs. There seemed to be so many. She led me to different areas. She showed me things, sexual things, that were happening. I felt as if my unconscious mind was making them up. They didn't seem real. She took me to the garage and showed me more. I won't believe these things. Shelli stays very accessible now. She comes out as soon as I start to play a tape.

The following day, as I lay down and closed my eyes, Shelli came out without the use of a tape:

Shelli takes me down the basement steps of my grandparents' house. It is dark and a little scary. We start toward the back where there is a storage room that has always frightened me. Before we get there, we come face-to-face with the devil. I am so terrified that everything disappears. I cannot play the "Transformation Now" tape as I planned. Shelli is more distant now. I think I have let her down by not seeing what she wants to show me. She still will come give me a hug, but now I must listen to the tapes alone.

This image of the devil—red cape, pitchfork, and all—scared me to death, and I didn't know what to make of it. I'd later realize that often the first time a memory emerged, the images that came up were metaphors. This became a pattern: the metaphor first, and, when I was ready, the actual memory. At times, it would take several sessions of seeing the same scene. Each one progressively having more detail and less metaphor. Sometimes this would all happen in a matter of days and other times over the course of months. I often needed to let an image settle for a while before being ready to see more.

For many years I had distanced myself from the concept of God and angels. It wasn't that I didn't believe, but with my Catholic upbringing and then my introduction to metaphysics, there was still a lot of confusion around the subject. With my renewed interest in metaphysics, I was beginning to feel more connected, at least to my angels.

I called on the angels as I prepared to go back and confront the devil. They did not let me down. This time it was easy to face the evil being that stood before me. With my courage worked up and my angelic protection in place, I swatted him away, knowing he was not real. He simply disappeared.

Shelli led me down the steps and into the back room of my grandparent's basement again. We turned on the light and I saw my maternal grandfather. I asked him to tell me what he knew. We went to the garage of my childhood home and we saw a family member sexually abusing me. Grampa came in and caught him.

None of that felt real. It was as if my grandfather thought I'd be satisfied if he merely showed me something. My gut correctly told me my relative was innocent of this deed.

The term "inner child" has been thrown around a lot, joked about, and even parodied. However, my inner children turned out to be very real. Not only were they alive, but they were actively influencing and governing my life. As a sensitive child, each time I was abused, demeaned, or hurt in any way, the child I was at that moment froze in time. These children never developed, never grew, but were always there. Over the years, I discovered I had hundreds of these frozen children guiding, and often controlling, every aspect of my life. I believe everyone has inner children to some degree. They can often stay secretly hidden, quietly exerting influence over a person's entire life, and no one is the wiser. That was not the case for me.

We each have our own way of dealing with abuse and painful issues. For some, the abuse or pain strengthens them and pushes them to overcome and achieve above and beyond what they otherwise would have. Others, like me, internalize it, hide it, and hope to keep it safely stowed away in some deep, dark part of ourselves. But all those things I stowed away were still alive inside me, not buried away to never be seen again. These were my inner children, my frozen children.

CHAPTER 8

Therapy Continues

THE EVENTS THAT FOLLOWED MY NEXT time on Apollonia's vibration table are still vivid in my mind. Driving home after my session I felt a small child, a year or two old, sitting on my lap. Although I couldn't see anything, there was a strong presence and the sense of a ghost-like image. Before arriving home, children of all ages were coming out. The next morning, in meditation, there must have been fifteen or more inner children, each frozen in their time, joining me. My meditation turned into a time of getting to know the children and answering their questions: Where were they? Could they live here with me? Were they safe? This was all so new to me. Did these children really exist? Was this how life was going to be from now on? I wasn't sure what to make of it all.

The hardest child to get to know was the three-year-old. She was difficult to bring out and seemed to have a great deal of anger. The seven-year-old was incredibly sweet and seemed bright and cheerful (she may have been there when I talked with Shelli the past week). She told me there was no six-year-old, she was both. With a sneaking suspicion I'd see a six-year-old later, I accepted her explanation. They were quite protective of one another.

With all the frozen children being so keyed up, it was difficult to sleep that night so I decided to go down to the living room to watch some television. Looking downward, I was surprised to find myself nursing an infant that I could see and feel yet I knew was not truly there. The frozen children were still coming out. They were so excited and active that by morning, I'd have given anything to have five minutes to myself.

The frozen children went to work with me that day. With children of all ages from tots to teenagers "walking" around my office, it was difficult to focus on my work. They weren't physically there and no one else could see them, but I sensed them and could almost make out the outlines of their invisible bodies. To me, they were there and they were real. As the day went on the children seemed to fade a bit and by afternoon I began to relax.

That evening at home, getting ready to prepare dinner, a couple of my inner teenagers came to talk to me. They said the little ones had a lot more to tell, but they didn't know what it was. Awaking from a dream that night, I sensed the three-year-old wanted to show me something. We agreed to listen to a tape, but when we tried, my tape recorder would not work. Later, it became apparent how powerful these children were. If one didn't want something to come out, she seemed to have the ability to manipulate electronics.

By the end of the week the children were getting harder to

reach. I'd seek them out—I still had lots of questions about what was happening—but they were more distant, not coming to me in the strong way they had been a few days earlier. This was an emotional time. Feelings of anger, doubt, and hopelessness were surfacing. Something was locked deep inside. I wondered if I'd ever be able to break through the walls I'd built and find out what it was. My weekly sessions with Apollonia helped to center me, but I was anxious to understand everything that was happening.

Feeling desperate that weekend, I begged the universe for help and pleaded for strength to see me through whatever was to come. Throughout the weekend I dealt with emotional ups and downs by praying, asking for help, and thanking the universe for the information received. Waking up Sunday morning I felt a sense of peace and calm I'd never known before. I didn't know where it came from, but I was thankful for this bit of tranquility. Asking my angels to send me a sign, I was hoping that something had been released and this peace would last. That was not the case as immediately a picture of a cartoon character popped into my head. The character was trying to pry a lid off a jar. I couldn't have gotten a clearer answer. My journey had barely begun.

CHAPTER 9

The Devil Revealed

O N THE WAY HOME FROM MY third session with Apollonia, I stopped by the grocery store. Everything was amazingly vivid, as if I possessed a new pair of eyes. Instead of seeing rows and aisles, each individual box and can leaped out in intense detail. Everything was much more vibrant than normal - it was like looking at a 3D picture where things jump out at you. My vision had become ten times sharper and colors were brighter and more alive. My vibration seemed to be at a whole new level. This temporary heightened awareness followed several of my sessions.

Between therapy sessions, I continued to spend as much time as I could interacting with my frozen children. With the help of the tapes, the children were again joining me on a regular basis now, but still the resolve I sought wasn't coming. I seemed to be finding more questions than answers. There was definitely a secret hidden deep inside, but I had no clue as to what it was. Some mornings I'd wake up with my stomach in knots. One of those days my stomach stayed in knots all day long. That night I heard the garage door open. Since no one else was home, or expected home, I went to investigate but could find nothing. Suspecting my angels were sending me a message, I decided to lie down.

When first starting to work with my inner, frozen children, I'd often get a feeling something was coming to the surface. Lying on my bed, memories or insights would arise. At the time, the wall lamp above my bed didn't work, except when something came up. As soon as a memory was released, the light would pop on of its own accord. You know the old expression, "a light bulb went off in her head." For me, this was the universe's way of confirming the accuracy of my memories and insights. Eventually my husband got around to fixing the light, and that was when the garage door began to open all by itself. It was as if the Universe was telling me "It's time to OPEN UP!"

As soon as I went upstairs, lay down, and closed my eyes, a long-forgotten memory came up and the images flowed. Several children, mostly older than I with the exception of one younger boy on the glider, were playing in the back yard of my childhood home. One of the older kids picked up a rock and threw it at me. Seeing it coming, I ducked and it missed me, but hit the younger boy, knocking him off the glider. The adults, who were chatting at the picnic table on the other side of the garage, heard the commotion and came quickly. One of the bigger boys pointed to me, claiming I'd thrown the rock. The little boy lay on the ground bleeding as I was sent to my room. Apparently he was fine, but my young mind imagined he was dead. Another dreadful moment that would be held deep inside by a newly born frozen child.

Apollonia owned a healing center in an old brick, ranch style home and as the months passed, she introduced me to other healers she worked with. One worked with light and sound; another was a network chiropractor. Both therapies were helpful in bringing my long-repressed memories to the surface. My desire to heal was strong, and I continued to work on my healing at home between sessions. Many days were full of emotional release and upheaval. One of the memories that surfaced at home after a light and sound session was especially traumatic for me.

The scene in my grandparent's basement came up again. This time the devil metaphor was gone and the actual memory emerged. I was only a couple of months old and my grandfather had taken me for a walk outside. When we returned to the house, we entered through the side door into the basement. Now, once more in my grandparent's basement, he took me to the dark back room, a storage area that ran across the width of the house with a door on either end. Grampa was sitting on some crates and had me lying on his lap. Taking off my diaper, he began to touch me. By this time, I was viewing the scene from above my body. Soon, I could hear my grandmother calling to my grandfather and that was all I saw, but it was enough. The devil had been revealed and it was my grandfather.

Shock, denial, disbelief, rationalization, and finally acceptance, then more denial, doubt, and not wanting to believe. These were just a few of the stages I went through as my repressed memories rose to the surface.

CHAPTER 10

My Grandfather

RELATIONSHIPS ARE FUNNY AND OFTEN COMPLICATED. Before the repressed memories surfaced, thoughts regarding my grandfather were only loving. Throughout my childhood in New York my grandparents lived about ten miles away and faithfully made the trek to our house twice a week. Every Sunday they spent the day with my family, often bringing a standing rib roast for dinner. We all enjoyed this meal, but none more than Grampa who was the happy recipient of the fat scraps off everyone's plates. They always stopped by Hemstrought's Bakery on the way to our house and would come in with two shopping bags full of goodies. Besides the fresh Italian bread to go with dinner, we could expect ginger jelly cookies or frosted chocolate squares, and always two white bakery boxes tied with white string. These contained the half-moons (a large chocolate cake like cookie with half chocolate and half vanilla frosting), our favorite cookies.

Grampa tended to hang out with the youngsters more than the adults. He took us on long walks "uptown" to the shopping district, or to the playground, or sometimes we'd go for a ride in his Buick. He never drove anything but Buicks and he rarely drove them at more than twenty-five or thirty miles per hour. After dinner, the children would gather on the steps to our basement and Grampa would sit and tell us stories. We called them his "snake stories" because our favorites all seemed to have a snake as the main antagonist.

He was also handy around the house and would help out by keeping the bushes trimmed, doing repairs, building things like a rack to keep our bikes orderly, and even a cabinet to lock medicines safely away from little hands. I am sure this was a big help to Mom, but it was also his way of keeping control over her.

Grampa dropped Grammy off for the day every Tuesday morning before he went downtown to open his liquor store. As if we didn't have enough dessert for the week, Grammy brought along a large jar of the most delicious fresh baked, chocolate chip cookies. Dad was away on business trips a lot and Mom's hands were full, so having Grammy there to help with the little ones and the house cleaning did give Mom some relief.

When the memory of being in the basement with my grandfather emerged, I was in shock. This did not happen. My grandfather would never do that to me, I told myself. He loved me. He wouldn't hurt me. I was a wreck, not wanting to believe these memories. The pictures wouldn't go away. They felt real, but I kept trying to deny it happened. I was only able to accept the reality of it by convincing myself that because I was so young, my grandfather must have believed I would never remember and it would not hurt me.

But the gate had been opened and over time more memories surfaced. In the next strong memory which came up, I was around a year or a year and a half old. Once again at my grandparents' house, this time in the dining room. Because I was teething, my grandfather was rubbing liquor on my gums (something commonly done in our family). He told my grandmother, "Mommy, we're going up to take a nap." He took me upstairs to his room (my grandmother's bedroom was on the main level) and gave me a bottle spiked with liquor. Soon I was passed out on the bed. Again, I watched the scene from above my body as my grandfather was all over me. I never could look at him committing the act. I'd see just enough to know what was going to happen next.

Although there's no tangible evidence, I have a strong feeling my mother went through much of the same abuse as I did when she was a child. Her fits of anger and rage fit the pattern of sexual abuse perfectly, something I know firsthand and often recognize in others who have suffered abuse and not yet dealt with it. Having this pent-up anger inside of her, it's not surprising how Mom reacted when, as a young child, I told her what Grampa was doing to me.

One of the strongest memories to resurface was from a time when I was three years old. My mother and I were in the den at home and she was struggling to get me dressed and ready to go to Grammy and Grampa's house. Fussing and resisting, I insisted I didn't want to go. When she questioned me as to why, I told her Grampa did bad things. When she asked what kinds of things, I revealed, "he puts the boy's thing in my bottom." This just set her off and made things worse. She blamed me and told me I was the bad one. She told me I was evil. Another frozen and angry child had been born.

CHAPTER 11

The Monster

THE HARDEST MEMORY OF ALL TO release came out in three phases over a matter of several months. Feeling something was close to coming up, I lay down as usual. The images came in vivid and clear. I was about four years old. The sun was shining brightly on this warm, beautiful day. It must have been a holiday of some sort because my brothers were in the garage putting red, white, and blue crepe paper in the spokes of their bikes, preparing to ride in the town parade. Our town sponsored parades for several occasions throughout the year and the participants began assembling where our house sat, on the corner of our small street and the main road running through town.

Excited, I ran into the house through the back door, down the hall, and up the stairs to the second floor. Once upstairs, I found myself fearfully backing down the long hallway. There was a monster coming toward me. The monster was around five feet tall, bulky, and walked awkwardly because it had a head between its legs. I could not see a face (again, I was given only what I could handle—another metaphor). The monster kept coming at me and I kept backing away, frightened. It grabbed me, picked me up, and threw me over the banister, down the stairs. The sensation of falling was so strong, I shot straight up in bed. It was such a compelling sensation that I was certain this incident truly happened. Yet it didn't make sense. Surely, I would have been hurt if this had actually taken place.

For weeks I attempted to figure out who the monster metaphor represented, putting various people in place of the monster, but nothing felt right. I had no idea who could have done this to such an innocent little girl.

In time, this scene would replay and still I saw the monster with the head between its legs. The first time I saw the scene, I felt the sensation of falling. The difference the second time was that I felt the sheer terror my four-year-old self experienced as she was being thrown over the railing and down the stairs.

It wasn't until a couple of months later, in the third resurfacing of this memory, that I was able to see the whole picture. By this time, I was working at *Aquarius*, a start-up new age newspaper, and I was having an especially emotional day. Something was close to the surface. I decided to go home early to try to release it. I didn't even make it home before the tears began and I found myself crying hysterically. The monster with the head between its legs was my mother, something that should have been easy to decipher (the head between the legs representing a mom giving birth), but up until this point I couldn't, or maybe wouldn't, see it. Still crying and terribly upset by this realization, I lay down when I arrived home and again the vision came up.

This time as I reached the top of the stairs it appeared my mother had been arguing with someone. Now I could see she was the angry one I was backing away from. The same scene played out, and she picked me up and threw me over the banister. Once more I felt myself falling, but I also saw something I hadn't seen before—being caught by the Archangel Gabriel and gently and safely being set down.

This memory was extremely disturbing to me, even more so than the memories of being abused by my grandfather. Had my mother in truth tried to kill me? I didn't want to believe it. I tried to rationalize it. She must have known what my grandfather was doing and she didn't want me to suffer through what I suspect she'd gone through. Or maybe I was simply picking up on her feelings and she was just angry and thought about doing it. It was too much to believe she would want to harm me.

It took me a long time to accept this as the truth. Years later, telling this story to my small Reiki class consisting of three psychics, I still couldn't convey the story without adding that I didn't know if it truly happened. In unison, they declared "It happened!" In my heart, I knew it was true, but I never wanted to believe it. The thought of my own mom hurting me was just too painful. Something more that needed healing. I'd had enough already to deal with. I tried to rationalize it. Maybe she had been in post-partum depression. Or maybe subconsciously she knew that she had been abused as a child and didn't want me to suffer the pain she had experienced all her life. Could she have been afraid that I would expose her father and what he had done to both of us? Would she then have to face her own childhood? I still don't have answers to these questions.

I suspect it was this incident that made me shut down everything. At the age of four, I repressed the memories, shut down psychically, turned off any otherworldly communication, and began to keep it all tightly guarded inside.

Survivors of childhood abuse of any kind often are gripped with feelings of being undeserving and unworthy of love or of anything good happening to them. Even though at the time of remembering this incident I was given the name of Archangel Gabriel as my rescuer, I couldn't believe I was important enough for an angel like Gabriel to help me. Divulging this story to my therapist, I changed my description of the angel from the well-known Archangel Gabriel to a more feminine (although angels have no sex), and unknown, angel named Gabrielle. I clung to that version of my experience for many years, not feeling worthy of the attention of an archangel.

Whether it be my nature, or due to my experiences in childhood, I am a doubter. I question everything about life. I demand proof, even though I tell myself, "When I believe it, then I will see it." I want to be the exception to that, wanting the universe to show me before I believe it. Yet, even when shown, doubt still persists. In my teen years, I was again shown evidence of the angels' protection, yet many times I would still deny the existence of non-physical entities.

As teenagers and pre-teens back in New York, my sisters and I were horse crazy and convinced Mom to let us take riding lessons. Each week Mom drove us to a riding stable out in the country where we progressed from trotting to cantering. One day, I was on a horse named Mike. It'd been raining all week and the practice ring was muddy and slick. As we began to canter around the ring, Mike slipped and lost his balance. All four legs went out from under him and he fell straight over on his side, going from vertical to horizontal in an instant. About twelve inches before he hit the ground, he did the impossible and was suddenly erect again. I never lost my seating or balance. No one saw this incident, except my younger sister. I don't know if she remembers it, but I will never forget it. Looking back now, the way he popped back up, there is no question in my mind an angel's hands pushed that horse back to a standing position and kept me from harm.

Angels and other non-physical entities are always around to offer help and guidance. It's very comforting to know they extend love and support without judgment or criticism. These days, I ask for their assistance often.

CHAPTER 12

An Almost Normal Life

REPRESSING THE MEMORIES OF THE SEXUAL, emotional, and physical abuse was a blessing and a curse for me. A curse in that it silently molded me into someone that hardly resembled who and what I might have become. Without a clue as to what happened to me, my life was unknowingly being strongly influenced by my past. It was a blessing in that it allowed me to go on with my life despite my past.

In most ways my life was normal, a good life with lots of happy memories. For a long time after the memories started to reemerge, it was hard to focus on anything but the pain and hurt. I hated my grandfather for what he'd done to me and my mother for not protecting me. Those memories seemed to consume me. Now, as wounds have healed, I'm able to look back at my childhood and focus on the happy times.

Summer was my favorite time. For several weeks each year, as I was growing up, the family would go to "camp." Camp was a place called Stiefvaters, located on Fourth Lake in New York's Adirondack Mountains. Our family always got the largest cabin and the only one which sat right on the lake shore, cabin number 10. In this rustic cabin we shared one small bathroom and doubled or tripled up in bed, just like at home.

For the kids it was all fun, but for Mom it was the same old work without the modern conveniences. I'm not sure if the old stove was wood-burning or gas, but it had to be lit with a match after lifting the iron cook plate off with an iron handle that hooked onto the burner. Mom was the chief dishwasher, cook, and the one who constantly swept the sand that collected on the wood floors throughout the day. The laundromat was off-site a few miles away. While Mom or Dad washed and dried loads of clothing, towels, and sheets, we amused ourselves collecting the shiny red mica abundant in the parking lot.

Preparing for camp was a project. Dishes, glassware, linens and such were not provided, so for a large family like ours (up to eight kids depending on how old I was at the time) there was a lot of packing to do. Some items were packed away each year and used only for this vacation, such as the silverware with red handles and the assortment of fancy china dinner plates, each one being unique. Setting the table for dinner each night, my sisters and I would fight over the plates, each hoping for our favorite. We all seemed to like the same bright floral patterns, while we shunned some of the less desirable designs with muted colors or patterns of wheat sheaths or baskets. Of course, we had to bring all the other necessities needed for a big family plus the extras used at the lake, such as towels, sunscreen, hats and such, as well as fishing poles, life preservers, water skis and the body board for those of us not coordinated enough to stay up on skis. We even brought along huge jugs of drinking water since the water out of the faucet came straight from the lake.

All of this was loaded into the station wagon or the boat being pulled by it, along with however many kids there were in the family at the time, each vying for a good spot in the car to settle into. There were no seat belts back then so we were sprawled anywhere we could find an open space.

We had a great swim area partially enclosed by a dock that consisted of a walkway with a large platform at the end. It was a great place for the kids to swim since the water didn't get too deep until the far side of the dock. Inside the swim area was a rustic log raft that looked like it'd been sitting in the water for a hundred years. All the kids dearly loved this raft and kept it in almost constant use. Once, three of us girls, along with a couple of the older boys at camp, took the raft out far past the dock. To our horror, the boys then jumped off and swam back to shore, leaving us stranded. It was getting dark as my dad begrudgingly came to our rescue with the motor boat and towed us back to the dock, scolding us for taking it out so far, not wanting to hear any excuses.

The motor boat was housed in the garage at home all year except for those weeks at camp. Every year we towed it behind the station wagon and watched Dad skillfully back the trailer into the water so the boat could be tied up to the dock near our cabin. Outings on the boat were one of my favorite pastimes while at camp. My dad usually drove, but sometimes he would let one of my brothers take control for a while. If we were far enough out, with no other boats around, even the girls might get a chance to steer. The moist air on my face and the wind in my hair gave me a feeling of abandon I rarely felt at home. Once each summer we would do a trip around the entire lake and through the channel connected to the next chain lake. Mom would cook chicken to make sandwiches on white bread slathered with butter. Sitting in the black and yellow scotch plaid cooler for hours, they were deliciously cold and moist by the time we ate them. Nothing ever tasted better.

Fourth Lake was part of the Fulton Chain Lakes. Going through the narrow channels that connected one lake to another was a special treat because of the low speed limits. That's when my dad would let two of us climb over the windshield and sit on the bow of the boat. One channel was not too far from our camp, and about halfway through, situated on one side of the narrow waterway, was a filling station and bait shop where we would refill the gas tanks and purchase worms for fishing. All the kids had their own fishing poles and we did a lot of fishing off the dock back at camp. We never ate the fish—our small catches wouldn't have made much of a meal anyway—just caught them, took them off the hook, and threw them back. One of the reasons I enjoyed fishing so much was because it was something we got to do with Dad.

Stiefvaters was a short walk from the small town of Inlet and my sisters and I would go there often. Directly across from the Stiefvaters' entrance was a little place full of enchanting gnomes and other figures for the yard. We always stopped to admire them as we started our walk into town. From there, we walked along the roadside, up and over a small hill. There were no sidewalks, but the road was not usually busy and we made our way along the shoulder next to the guardrail. The town itself was lined with shops filled with the most wonderful assortment of merchandise. It was easy to spend hours looking around and being overwhelmed by the goods that were so different from what we found in the stores at home. Most of the items were of the souvenir type, but to us they were all treasures. We always came home with a keepsake or two, favorites of mine being Indian dolls (Native American is more politically correct these days, but as a child we only knew to call them Indians), china animals, or giant lollipops.

Back in those days you had to make your own entertainment while at camp. There was not a television set anywhere on the property.

Most nights someone would build a campfire outside the lean-to by the lake. It sat on the opposite side of the property from cabin number 10, and the adults would sit around the fire and talk while the kids found sticks, stuck a marshmallow on top, and toasted up golden brown, gooey treats.

For cheap but fun entertainment, the campers liked to go to the town dump at night. That was when the bears came out scavenging for food. On any given night you could find a large crowd of people gathered around the smoldering piles of trash. When I was little, I'd cling to my dad's leg, peeking out to get a glimpse of the bears as they came closer and closer to the spectators. Finally, when they got too close, someone would snap a picture and the flash sent the bears scampering down the hill and back into the woods.

School let out the first or second week of June and we started back after Labor Day, giving us a three-month break. To me, school was always something forced on me and not something looked forward to, so summers were a welcome interruption. We lived on a little dead-end street, but there were lots of youngsters and one of the places they tended to congregate was our side yard. As a child, I thought it was plenty big. It was only seeing it again as an adult that I realized how small it was. On the back corner was our swing set, the usual metal backyard set with two swings, a glider, and a slide at the end. The support bar that ran between the legs also served as a great place to do gymnastics and hang upside down. Over the years, that old swing set got more than its share of use. It also served as second base for our frequent games of kick ball. This was a neighborhood favorite and our yard was the right size and shape to play the game. Home base was at the front of the yard just inside the row of short shrubs which separated the yard from our quiet street. First base was a worn dirt spot by the row of matching trees that divided our yard from the neighbors, and the big old shade tree next to the garage worked fine for third base.

The other attraction in this little yard was the homemade sand box that sat below the shade tree. It consisted of four wood planks with diagonal boards positioned across the corners. I'm not sure if it was already a fixture when my parents bought the home or if it was built by Grampa, or perhaps even my father who did turn out a project every now and then. However it got there, it got plenty of use, as we spent a lot of time in that sand box building roads and running our little cars over them. A real treat was when Kenny Marsh would stop by to help with our road system before going to the house to meet with my brothers.

Kenny was four years older than I and the only one of my brother's friends that took the time to play with us outside a group setting. He was smart and creative, and also a bit of a philosopher—the kind of person, as I looked back later, that I could imagine reading his poetry in a smoky college coffee house. I loved to listen in on what, to my young mind, were deep and meaningful conversations he engaged in with my brothers. I was just six or seven, but I adored Kenny. He may have been my first crush.

The kids from our street and a few other nearby houses had favorite spots to play, depending on what the game was. Whereas kick ball was played in our yard, red rover was played in the street between our house and the Benson's house across the road. The neighbors behind us maintained a great, flat yard with an almost stage-like end on it and on summer evenings we could count on having up to twenty neighborhood kids congregating to play outdoor games. This group changed from night to night but included kids of all ages from kindergarteners to junior high school age, both boys and girls. We spent hours playing tag, spud, blacktown-blacktown, red light-green light, mother-may-I, and a variety of other games, only breaking up as it got too dark to see and parents shouted out their front doors or came looking for their kids.

Different groups would get together during summer days and I'm fairly certain Kenny Marsh also spearheaded what I'll call "The Gaffney House Gaffe." Mrs. Gaffney lived in a stately old house with a large additional lot on the side. I remember the house with its tall columns on the front porch as being dark and not well maintained. The yard was usually unkempt and in need of mowing and a good allover trim. Although she rarely made an appearance, my young mind guessed Mrs. Gaffney must have been at least one hundred years old or so. The Gaffney house faced College street, as did Kenny Marsh's house. We often cut through the neighbors' backyards to reach Kenny's house and if we continued on we'd reach Mrs. Gaffney's large backyard, which was as equally unkempt and overgrown as the front. There was some sort of long structure in the back—maybe an old chicken coop—that had long since been abandoned. The building itself was fairly low, so it wasn't too difficult to climb on top of the roof, a good vantage point to be sure there was no one in the backyard to spot us, an unlikely event since she lived alone and stayed indoors most all the time.

Coming off the back of Mrs. Gaffney's house was a rather large covered patio with lots of nooks and crannies, as well as old furniture. One day as a group of us neighborhood children were exploring it, someone came up with a brilliant idea. Mrs. Gaffney never used this area and it would make a perfect clubhouse for us. We scoped out the place and everyone settled on a spot that would be their own designated area. Of course, the older ones got first choice and took prime locations such as the steps, the almost empty storage closet, the old dusty glider, and so forth. The younger kids were happy to settle for an empty corner or an area along the planter wall, just glad to be included. We held our first official club meeting, decided on a time to meet back, and we each went home to gather the items that would make our designated spots special—books, games, baseball cards, cars, dolls, and so on. At the agreed upon time we returned with our personal treasures, along with some supplies to tidy the place up, and settled into our spaces.

This was an ideal gathering place for us for several days. It ended one evening when there was a knock at our front door and my parents opened it to find "Big John Law" standing there. "Big John Law" was the title the town's kids bestowed upon the lone policeman in our little community of less than two thousand. He'd received a complaint from Mrs. Gaffney that some children had been trespassing on her property. We, along with the families of the rest of the children involved, were warned to remove our personal items and not to disturb Mrs. Gaffney again.

We didn't get into any real trouble over this, probably just a stern lecture on respecting other people's property. I'd imagine most of the parents kind of laughed to themselves, shook their heads, and wondered, "What the hell were those kids thinking?"

We may have been banned from Mrs. Gaffney's house, but that didn't stop us from going to Gaffney's field. Gaffney's field was hidden a fair ways behind the Gaffney house by a thin row of trees. The narrow band of trees encircled the entire field which extended behind the houses across the road from ours, all the way down Cleveland Place, then alongside Oriskany Creek at the end of the road, and around to the back of the houses on the next street over—about a two-block area. It was a big field and its only purpose, as far as I could tell, was to host a large horse show each year.

Access to the horse show was gained through the entrance situated on the empty lot next to the Gaffney house. Of course, you were required to pay an admission fee if you went through the front gate. The neighborhood children never went through the front gate. It was much quicker and easier to cut through backyards. From our house, all we had to do was cut across the Benson's yard, through Andy Roy's yard next door, then into the narrow, wooded area and through the barbed wire fence, already stretched out by our scores of previous visits. This dumped us into the only place in the field we cared about being anyways—the pony rides. Each year, my sisters and I, along with our friends, would pick out our favorite ponies and we would ride them as many times as we could, going back and forth to scrounge up more money. If we didn't have the money, we were happy to watch the other kids ride as we petted the ponies that were resting.

We would go back and forth, from home to field and field to home, countless times over horseshow weekends. One year, Andy Roy must have gotten a bit tired of all this traffic through his yard. He was good-natured about it, but at some point we found a black cable in the grass, stretched across our path. Andy warned us the cable was electrified and we would likely be killed instantly if we stepped on it. Giving him a questioning look, I dutifully jumped over the cable. The cable didn't keep anyone off Andy Roy's grass, but we did approach it cautiously. I continued to carefully jump the cable each time I crossed the yard until I finally could stand it no longer. I had to know. Surely he was fibbing. I stood there looking at the cable, debating. Do I dare? The need to know overtook me and I put the tips of my toes on it. Nothing. I was safe. Just another grown-up fib. Smiling I went on my way jingling the change in my pocket and anticipating my next pony ride.

I wonder how many times Andy Roy watched neighborhood children jump over that cable. I wonder how many children continued to jump the cable and how many ended up testing his story. Either way, I'm sure he got a good laugh out of it. As for me, I had discovered the lie. Next time I wouldn't be so gullible.

CHAPTER 13

Grammy And Grampa's House

MOM ONCE TOLD ME I DIDN'T like to spend the night at Grammy and Grampa's house when I was very young. After recovering the memories, this made sense considering what happened in my early years. Once the memories were repressed at age four, the fun aspects of visiting Grammy and Grampa took over and I even looked forward to spending the night.

They'd purchased their house when first married in the 1920s, and when their family started growing they finished off the upper level. The house was entirely different from the home we lived in and had features I thought were amazing. In the kitchen was a three-foot-tall door, that opened to a trash chute leading to the basement (I've heard my oldest brother fell down this when he was a toddler, but my grandmother waited years before telling Mom). The main level bathroom had a small round access door in the floor that served as a laundry drop to the basement, but for the kids' purpose it was a communication portal. Above the kitchen sink was a buzzer used to call the family to dinner or to warn the children to settle down. On the corner of the house was an insulated compartment with doors on the inside and outside where the milkman would pick up empty bottles and drop off a fresh supply of milk twice a week.

The basement was a favorite place to play. It was long and narrow with Grampa's work area and storage tables on one side and end. There was an old pot belly stove used to burn trash and an early electric refrigerator, which looked like an old-fashioned ice box, and was nothing like the modern appliance in our kitchen at home. The opposite side was lined with wood pallets where I'm sure a lot of things were stored, but mostly I remember the boxes we'd play with. (There were always lots of empty liquor boxes brought home from his retail store. No one would get upset if we destroyed them, as often happened.) In the center of the basement was an island formed by the washer and dryer, more pallets and storage, and above all of that, hanging from the rafters were bags and bags of wedding and prom dresses that belonged to Mom and her three sisters, as well as tuxedos and military uniforms that had previously been worn by Mom's two brothers. Across the width of the back was the long and narrow, scary storage room with a door on each end. As youngsters, my sisters and I were afraid of this room and would only run through it on a dare. I don't know if any of my sisters had reason to fear the room, or if maybe they just picked up on my fear.

My favorite things in the basement were the two wooden swings Grampa hung years ago for his own children. The swings, which faced one another with ten to fifteen feet between them, were suspended from the ceiling beams by chain. The large hooks at the top and bottom allowed us to adjust the seats to most any height. My siblings and I would spend hours in the basement playing the games we concocted just for the swings. We'd take one of the empty boxes and try to kick it past the other person as they sought to defend their territory while staying in motion. Another much-loved game was "dare devil." We'd have to get the timing of our swings just right. With two of us working up as much speed as we could, the third would try to run across our path from pallet to pallet without getting hit by our extended legs.

The second floor of their home was also filled with treasures. The sloping roof formed side attic storage areas accessed by child-sized doors. These areas were small, but full of magnificent treasures like my uncles' old metal army men and the dolls my mom and her sisters played with while growing up. There was an open play room area and down the hall were the bedrooms. My grandfather's bedroom was on the right, his bottom dresser drawer loaded with simple jigsaw puzzles that we never tired of putting together. Across the hall was the boys' room with two old iron twin beds. The large room at the end of the hall with two double beds belonged to my mother and my aunts when they were children. The center window looked out over the covered front porch and onto the street. On either side of the window were small built-in dressing tables attached to tiny, curtained closets, made even smaller by the sloped ceilings.

Sleeping at my grandparents' house was strange for me. Together, with my three sisters, we would snuggle into the beds and wait. My grandfather never failed to come in after we'd settled down and he'd stand in the doorway watching us. Shutting my eyes before he got there, I'd pretend to be asleep, but I could feel his presence. After what seemed like a very long time I'd finally hear him turn and walk the short distance down the hall to his own room, slippers flopping on the linoleum floor. I could finally close my eyes and go to sleep for real. But nights were different at my grandparents' house. No dreams, no tossing and turning, no waking up in the middle of the night. I'd close my eyes and open them a moment later and it was morning. This amazed me as such a strange phenomenon, but I now wonder if it was purely part of my self-protection.

We had great times visiting Grammy and Grampa. I would guess Grampa, who was of Irish descent, stood around 5'6" tall and was a little round about the middle. On either side of his bald head was a mixture of gray and black hair, and he wore dark rimmed glasses. Whenever he was home, he immediately exchanged his shirt and trousers for a plaid bathrobe which he wore only loosely wrapped around by the belt, leaving his sleeveless white undershirt and boxer shorts exposed. This was just Grampa; we were all used to that.

Grampa was all about the children, again taking us for walks or driving the short distance to the city zoo where we'd stop and feed the deer. Whenever the ice cream truck came around, he'd give us each a dime to buy a cone. Of course, no visit was complete without at least one of his fabulous sodas—ginger ale over vanilla ice cream. I loved my grandparents and felt loved by them. Sometimes it felt like they were they only ones that did love me. I guess that was why it was so hard for me to accept that my grandfather could have done anything to hurt me.

As we were preparing to move to Atlanta, Grampa gave me three gifts. Knowing I was interested in art and photography as hobbies, he gave me a beautiful set of long-treasured art books. These were made even more special to me when I saw his name and address beautifully written in calligraphy on the inside cover. He also gave me his vintage camera with folding black bellows. The third gift was one I know was special to him—a brownie camera that belonged to his oldest son who was killed when the military jet he was piloting crashed. It is not uncommon for a sexual predator to single out one child in a family. Grampa made me feel like I was one of his favorites and his gifts seemed to confirm it. As far as I know, he didn't give parting gifts to any of my seven siblings. At the time, I treasured these gifts. Later, they began to feel like hush money.

My grandfather had been dead for almost fifteen years when I began to remember the abuse, so I wasn't able to confront him. I released my anger toward him by physically attacking him in my dreams and writing letters filled with cursing and rage. I knew at some point I would have to let all the rage and hatred go, not for him, but for my own well-being. But letting go of all that anger inside took some time.

I loved my grandmother. She had a good heart and, in contrast to my mother, I can't bring to mind a single instance where she ever got mad or even raised her voice to me or anyone else. She was devoted to my grandfather, calling him "my boyfriend." She kept a clean house and cooked and baked. I don't recall her having any hobbies. She didn't drive and spent much of her time at home when she wasn't at our house on Sundays and Tuesdays. If she wanted to go somewhere, Grampa would drive her, or for shopping downtown, the bus line was nearby.

Looking back, it was as if she were put on earth to play a supporting role, to be around to take care of everyone's basic needs while we all played out the drama of our karma. I doubt she had any clue as to what my grandfather did to me or to my mother, her oldest child. She seemed content with her role and I've never felt anything but love for her.

Grampa died the year I was married. Without Grampa, Gram was lonely wandering around the house by herself, so a couple of years later she accepted Mom and Dad's offer to come live with them in Georgia. While Mom may have thought this was a good idea, it wasn't all love and joy. Mom clung to every injustice ever done to her or her family, letting it consume her life. She still had a lot of rage inside and continued to fly off into her rants when anything upset her. I remember my grandmother looking so puzzled and commenting to me, "She never used to be like this." Grammy was in her eighties by then. I'm not sure if she forgot Mom's explosions or if Mom had kept them hidden when Grammy and Grampa were around.

After a couple more years, Gram's health was deteriorating. She was in and out of the hospital and I'd stop by to see her on my way home from work. On my last visit to her she wasn't aware of her surroundings or my presence. Staring off into empty space, she would utter something every now and then, such as, "I've never seen anything like it." I speculated as to whether she was seeing the afterlife or remembering something from her childhood.

The morning following that visit, while at work at my dad's pharmaceutical company, my left arm and shoulder suddenly started to hurt. The pain was strong and it was uncomfortable to move it even a little bit. I'd been working at my desk when this began, not doing anything strenuous. The aching kept up for a while and then went away as quickly as it had started. Soon after, my brother came in to tell me the hospital had called to say my grandmother had died. Now I understood where the pain came from. It wasn't the first time I'd felt someone else's pain and I hoped my discomfort had at least eased my grandmother's suffering somewhat.

I had always felt a connection with and love for my grandmother, but her death did not have a huge emotional impact on me. Yes, I would miss her, but it was her time. I was busy working and raising two small children. It wasn't until several years later, when I was in a healing session with my energy worker, Flenn, that I began to feel a new, even stronger connection to Grammy. Flenn told me someone else (a non-physical presence) was there with us. I knew immediately who it was because my grandmother's image had just flashed through my mind. Although I never thought of her as a particularly strong woman when she was alive, I knew it took a lot of love and strength for her to get through to me in my current state of emotional upset.

She had one simple but powerful message that I will never forget: DO NOT DOUBT YOURSELF. This was a message I needed to hear and I was grateful to have received it.

CHAPTER 14

The Newspaper

FTER SEVERAL YEARS, DAD'S COMPANY HAD grown, he had a board of directors to deal with, and problems were mounting. Those problems were resolved by selling the company to a larger pharmaceutical outfit. The new owners were out of state and kept me on to manage one division of the company, a group I'd been acting as general manager for in addition to my other duties. As for Glenn, he and his dad had started their own business and were working hard to get it off the ground. With Glenn's business not yet bringing in a large salary, my paycheck was important. There was some animosity between the new owners and my family, so the situation was a bit rocky for a while, but I felt like I had no choice but to stay on.

All of this was happening as I was reconnecting with metaphysics. I continued to work at my job, running the company division with a group of fifteen or so people reporting to me. Working for the new company was fine and they seemed to be happy with my performance. But things at home didn't feel right. Our kids were getting older (Alix was eight and Adam was ten) and I felt like I wasn't giving them the time they deserved. On top of that, I was dealing with my emerging memories. After a year at the new company, I told Glenn how I was feeling, and he was ready to support me in whatever decision I made.

The next day at work I gave my notice, not sure of what I was going to do. But I knew something needed to change. An hour or so later, a beautiful bouquet of flowers was delivered to my desk. There was no card enclosed, simply a magnet with the name of the florist shop. Glenn was not in the habit of sending flowers and I hadn't yet called him to let him know I'd given my two-week notice. Puzzling over where they'd come from, I was certain the mysterious flowers were my confirmation from the universe that I was making the right decision. I was so excited that at lunch I went to see Gloria at the metaphysical bookstore. She was in the process of kicking off a New Age newspaper, *Aquarius*, and desperately needed help. Telling her I'd given my notice and relaying the flower mystery, she looked at me and said, "This morning I asked Spirit to send me someone, and to send them today." She offered me the position as office manager on the spot and I had my new job. I later found out Glenn had sent the flowers, but I firmly believe the universe played a hand in leaving out the card and setting into motion the events that followed.

I enjoyed my new job as the *Aquarius* office manager. The money wasn't what I was used to making, but it was nice not to be under so much pressure all the time. Working with Gloria, I saw the trust she placed in the universe to take care of everything for her. Each day I learned more about the metaphysical community and what they had to offer.

When I joined *Aquarius*, I was still heavily into releasing memories and working with my inner children who were turning out to be powerful forces. Not only did they have control of my emotions, they also seemed to have the ability to control my computer. We were working late one night, trying to make deadline for our first edition. Computer issues kept popping up and one crucial program would not work at all. I was tired and ready to go home, feeling the need to do some release work. But deadline was approaching to get the paper out on our scheduled date, so I kept trying. After a couple of hours, I determined it wasn't going to happen that night, so I decided to go home, relax, and release. As soon as that decision was made the program mysteriously started to work, keeping me busy at the office for another couple of hours. It was as if some inner frozen child, who did not want me doing my release work, had gained control over my computer. With the threat of going home, the computer program was freed to allow me to stay and continue my office tasks and delaying my inner work.

CHAPTER 15

More Children Emerge

MY TIME WITH APOLLONIA AND THE practitioners at her center was amazing and started me on my path to healing. As much as I loved those sessions, the universe was guiding me in a new direction. My sessions with Flenn were powerful and I did a lot of clearing. When he did his energy healing I could feel a force moving through various parts of my body, releasing blocked energy. He taught me to go to my heart to look for answers. We experienced many powerful sessions together and I valued his guidance.

Flenn often worked with Anyaa, a licensed clinical counselor, more mainstream than Apollonia, but with a metaphysical slant not typically found in the conventional medical community. I was still having difficulty coping with all the memories that had come up and dealing with anger and depression, while trying to maintain a job and give my children the support they needed. It wasn't easy and I wanted to be there for my family, but all these issues seemed to be consuming me. Flenn suggested I work with Anyaa.

Anyaa showed me ways to release my anger. One thing she taught me was how to get in touch with my feelings and to release them. I'd lie on a mat on the floor while she put on music and encouraged me to let my inner sounds and feelings come out. This was the first time I'd ever been given permission to let these out and releasing them was a breakthrough for me. Sorrowful moans and groans erupted in a volume I didn't know I was capable of reaching.

As I released emotions from deep inside myself, I found that what was churning within was more than anger, it was a full-blown rage that needed emancipation. Anyaa suggested I get a plastic baseball bat and an old pillow or cushion. She gave me three rules: 1) I couldn't destroy any property, 2) I wasn't to hurt myself, and 3) I wasn't to hurt anyone else. Following these three rules I could use the bat to pound on the cushion and unleash my anger. For the next several years I used the exercise she taught me on a regular basis, unmercifully letting loose my anger, screaming at God, the angels, my mother, my grandfather, and anyone or anything else that came up, all while pounding the bat with all my might on the poor, innocent pillow.

As I continued therapy with Anyaa, the inner children kept emerging. I'd come to find out there were two categories of children—the inner or frozen children, who'd been traumatized or hurt in some way, and the dissociated children who'd taken on their own personalities to protect me or help me handle situations. These dissociated children didn't completely split away from me. While they influenced my behavior, they never took over totally as in Dissociative Identity Disorder (Multiple Personalities). The following italicized items are entries from my journal at the time. Non-italicized notes are added for clarification:

2/16 Sara – eight years old. "Keeper of the Secrets." Has a trunk to keep things in. We agreed to keep the trunk unlocked so memories can come out as they are ready to. Found her an alternate job—keeping the flower gardens.

2/17 Elley – four years old. Stands against a door, keeping it guarded. She keeps me from discovering the feelings and thoughts of the others. She doesn't like Anyaa because she tries to make me tell what the others have to say. We talked about this being okay now. Asked her what else she likes to do—color. I promised to get her art supplies. She will do pictures for us.

2/20 Sam - I'm not sure if Sam is female or male or both. I can't tell her exact age but I would guess twelve to fourteen. She eats constantly and is very obese. She stays in a kitchen and dining room area. She basically ignores me. Won't answer my questions.

2/20 Brenda is a sweet child, age six. I found her swinging and singing. She was somewhat scared and jumped off the swing as I approached. Her job is to keep the innocence (I think maybe she was protecting not only my innocence, but the inner children's as well).

2/20 "The Screaming One." I went looking for this one because of the sound I heard inside myself earlier this night.

I found her with arms and legs shackled to a cave-type wall. Her long hair was dirty and stringy, her clothes old and worn. When asked her name she screamed she had no name. When asked how old she was, she screamed she had no age. She holds the torture. She yelled at me to leave and tried to project evil things at me. (It was not so much that I could see evil, but more of an overwhelming feeling of evil and darkness.)

2/21 Sybil (named herself after the movie character). About twelve years old. Pretty, blond, very nice. She acts as the coordinator and sometimes peacemaker with all the others. She has offered to guide me around in meeting the others.

2/23 Karen – Sybil led me up dark circular stairs to find her. She was sitting in a small tower-like area with her head to her knees, crying. She is fifteen. She feels things are hopeless. Stays in the tower to stay away from her mother's screaming and yelling.

2/28 Lynn – I first saw Lynn about a month ago. She's a sad child about four years old. She seems to be an inner child and not a dissociated personality (just a feeling—it wasn't always easy to tell the difference). *She stays in the same place as the other inner children, but keeps to herself.*

(conversation with Lynn)

How are you Lynn?

Sad.

Why are you sad?

The bad people.

Who are the bad people?

Can't tell.

Lynn, I am here to protect you. We have a lot of people helping us. The bad people can't hurt you anymore. Do you understand?

Can't tell anyone.

It's okay to tell. Telling will help make the bad people go away. Can you tell me what they did?

Hurt me. I don't like them.

> *Do you want to tell the bad people how you feel?*
> *It's okay to get angry at them.*

> *Stop.*

I decided to put on headphones and listen to some music in hopes of bringing up some memories, to see what Lynn couldn't say. Lynn always seems to be in raingear, so I focused on that:

> *I see myself standing in front of the kitchen door. My grandfather is helping me on with my coat. He is going to give my mother a break and take me out for a drive. Next, I am sitting in the front seat of his car, looking up at him. I am quiet, not smiling.*

> *We go inside a building, like a cave or basement. A very pretty lady is putting a white gown on me. She hands me down to someone, maybe my grandfather. I am laid on a table, I think my arms are restrained. I am forced to drink from a chalice—it is blood. I cough and choke. I think after that there is some kind of sexual act.*

> *This memory doesn't seem exactly real, but I think it has some significance. I'm just not sure.*

> *I call on Sybil for assistance. Maybe she can show me someone who has more information on this. She leads me up a path to a room. Inside is a small child sitting with her back to me. She is wearing a simple white gown. When she gets up and turns around I can see she is carrying a doll*

that looks exactly like her. The doll is also in a white gown and has a knife in her chest and blood splattered on her gown. The child's gown is also splattered with blood. The child is about four years old and is called Angel.

In the weeks and years to come I would learn much more about Angel's story.

CHAPTER 16

Rescuing The Children

IN THOSE EARLY DAYS, WHEN I so desperately needed help and healing, it felt like I was being divinely guided from one person to the next. Each one offered something special and added to my healing. As I continued my work with Flenn, a lot of stuff was shifting and coming up and, at his suggestion, I began working with Marcelle, another licensed counselor. Marcelle's transpersonal psychotherapy sessions were a good compliment to the energy work that I was doing with Flenn.

Marcelle and I continued to work with my frozen children. She helped me create a special place in my heart to take them - a place where they could heal and be safe. When asked to imagine and create this space, the image of a large field came to me. We called this place "the meadow." The meadow boasted a large shade tree near the entrance and continued on as an open field. I would accompany the child (calling upon the angels to join us) to the meadow and hold or talk to them until they felt safe and understood that no one could hurt them while they were in the meadow. I'd let them know they could call to me if they needed me, and I'd hear them. When they were ready, the angels would guide them to their permanent home where their spirit would be returned to a state of pure light and love. The meadow was a magical place where a child could create anything and everything they desired. Over the years I would rescue countless children and take them to this beautiful field.

This journal entry is from one of the first rescues we did:

We rescued my six-year-old inner child today (this was my first time meeting her). She was so sad and alone. Her world was one of despair and hopelessness. Her loneliness and abandonment were so deep I couldn't help but cry as I held her and tried to connect with her.

The shield of protection she'd built around her heart was strong, almost impenetrable. It served her well to protect her all these years, but it also held in the pain and kept it from being released.

I held my hand over her heart and sent in light to soften the hard wall of protection. It began to break down and soften. Slowly, a bit at a time, I gained her confidence.

After resting for a while I took her to the meadow in my

heart where my two-year-old was already residing. In this
magical land she could heal and would be safe and loved.
No one would ever hurt her again.

But what about me? I went home with a heavy heart. This session really got to me. I'd been in therapy for a while now and it seemed as if I hadn't been able to feel the pain and suffering my inner children went through. Now, with the six-year-old, I could see how damaged she was, how much she must have suffered.

My emotions the rest of the day were heavy. I felt despair and loneliness. A hopelessness came over me—feelings of being nothing, that I didn't matter. I wanted to give up. Hadn't I already done away with these feelings?

Oh my God! I gasped at the sudden realization that these were not my feelings, these were the emotions of my frozen children. I'd worried about not connecting to the inner children's pain and now I understood their feelings were what I'd been experiencing my entire life! For the first time, I was able to identify the source of my emotions. But now what was I supposed to do with them?

The next couple of days were an emotional seesaw. My mood would plunge into darkness and despair and I'd forget the emotions belonged to a frozen child. Then I'd remember, go to the child to hold and comfort her, and reassure her she is safe and would not be hurt again. Things would be better for a while, then the feelings would come back up and I'd want to hang onto them. I was still claiming them as my emotions too, and I didn't want to let go. I'd spend a lot of time in the meadow comforting these children. The emotions would pass, relief would come, and I'd want to live again.

My frozen children had been controlling most every aspect of my life. Now I was learning to go inside and identify who was behind my problems and negative emotions. My life was being run by my inner children and my entire adult self was missing or held little control over my life. I wanted to let my inner adult take control, but this wasn't as simple as I'd hoped. At that point, I had no idea how many children were still frozen inside of me.

The following week I heard my six-year-old call to me. I stretched out on the bed and went inside my heart to the meadow expecting to find her upset. She wasn't. As I held her and talked to her I noticed there were now other children who'd gone to the meadow. They appeared as shadows to begin with, but they were close by and seemed to belong there. Focusing my attention on my solar plexus, I identified a five-year-old, an eight-year-old, and a twelve-year-old. I had met these frozen children in the prior week and now I talked to each one of them, letting them know I loved them and that this was their new home in my heart. It felt good to see them happy and content as they went off to play. Even the six-year-old was happy and playful. There was hope.

CHAPTER 17

The Priest

AS I CONTINUED MY HEALING WORK, more memories came out over the course of the next few weeks and months. Many of them were just snatches and hard to grab hold of. Sometimes I would try to embellish them and fill in the pieces. That technique never worked, and the stories I made up would quickly fade away. I reasoned if it truly was something that needed to be released and remembered, it would come to me clearly and stick with me over time. This is one of those memories:

> *I'm about seven years old. It must be winter because I have on my heavy coat. I'm in the church basement (where religion classes were held). I guess I left my hat or mittens*

in the classroom. It's not actually a classroom, but a narrow room at the back of the basement with stone walls and folding chairs. The basement has a lot of stone and funny passageways.

As I go back I see a priest. He stops me. I am scared, but I don't resist too much. He pulls me into a dark crevice. I am sitting on his lap with my back to his chest. He reaches with one hand and rubs against my vaginal area. He plays with his penis with the other hand, rubbing it underneath me.

He tells me God wants him to do this to me, but I mustn't tell anyone or God will punish me. When he finishes, I get up to leave. I'm not frightened or hurt—more numb. I let him do it to me. I accept it—this is what adults do to kids. You just have to let them.

But you mustn't talk about it.

My mother and father were devoted Catholics, Mom having been raised in the religion and Dad converting before they were married. Every Sunday, and on Holy Days of Obligation, we faithfully went to church, and my siblings and I attended Sunday school either before or after services. I didn't mind church as a youngster. We attended mass in a large, beautiful brick church built in the early 1900s, just majestic enough to humbly honor God. On the outside, it appeared as though it could have been three stories tall, but inside, save the balcony where the organist sat, was only one story with a grand cathedral ceiling. There were rows and rows of large wooden pews with kneelers that tucked out of the way when not in use. The large well-appointed altar was separated from the parishioners by a white marble railing with brass trim and included a gate in the center so the priests could enter after a procession. In front of the railing was a long pad to kneel on and receive holy communion. There was a marble pulpit, a marble altar, and behind that another large ornate marble altar that housed statues, candles, and other ceremonial items used during church services. Behind the altar and down each side of the church were beautiful stained-glass windows that told the story of Jesus, or his death—I don't recall exactly—but to me, they were mesmerizing.

When I was very young, I'd stare at the priest during mass as he stood in the pulpit giving his sermon. At the time, I didn't know what an aura was but there often appeared to be a halo around his entire head. While I still believe this priest to have been a truly good and holy man, I would later find out that not all priest's halos shined equally. Sexual predators have a way of picking out those children who are vulnerable. They have an uncanny knack for recognizing youngsters who are already victims of abuse, making those children more susceptible to further victimization. Apparently, I was no exception.

Church was something I was required to do. I never felt a particular attachment to the Catholic religion. Despite my catechism classes, there were a lot of things about Catholicism that didn't make sense to me, and as I got older I questioned them more and more. I doubted that God sent people to hell for eternity, without even a second chance. Was the Catholic religion really the only true religion as I had been taught? And what about the babies who died before they were baptized? It didn't seem fair that they went to purgatory (or maybe it was limbo), but the only way to get to heaven was if enough prayers were said for them. And what about all those unfortunate people who didn't even know about being baptized? It wasn't right not to let them into heaven. But then, from what we learned from the nuns, it didn't seem like many of us had much of a chance to reach heaven anyway.

We always seemed to be doing something that would send us right to hell.

By my mid-teens I'd pretty much dismissed the teachings of the church, but lacked concrete ideas of what to believe. At my parents' insistence, I continued to go to church every Sunday, sitting in the back and sneaking out to wander around the parking lot until services ended. I guess up until that point Mom and Dad believed there was still hope for me and my soul. They finally gave up and let their heathen daughter skip this mockery.

It wasn't until I moved away from home that Pam gave me my first taste of metaphysics and my strong spiritual beliefs began to form. The more I learned, the more it all made sense. Sure, there were still a lot of unanswered questions, but the concepts I grasped felt right to me. Reincarnation made sense. Instead of having one chance to get it right, growing and learning in each incarnation gave life more purpose. I'd never liked the idea of God being someone to fear. The portrayal of a loving God was easier for me to believe in. And what about the image of God sitting on a throne? It was hard to accept God as just a super-human being. There had to be more to the story.

I still don't have all, or even most of the answers, but I'm comfortable with what I do believe, knowing my knowledge will continue to grow and change throughout the rest of this life and eternity.

CHAPTER 18

Family Nonsupport

GLENN AND I HAD OUR SHARE of problems over the years. There were a lot of rough spots along the way to where we are now. I had my issues and I'm sure I wasn't easy to live with a lot of the time. He was not quite twenty-four when we married and still had a lot of maturing to do. Before we had our first child, during one of those tough times he told me, "We need to figure out some way to get a divorce." I was devastated. At the time, no one in my family had ever been divorced. I was going to be the one to fail. We managed to get through that period, experienced some good times, and endured some difficult times over the next few years, but we stuck together.

The next serious bump in our relationship came as the memories were resurfacing. By this time we were a family of four, I was a mess, and we were again on the verge of divorce. Glenn didn't know how to handle what I was going through. I used to tell him all the time, "It's not always about you," but that was exactly how he reacted. When I tried to talk to him about what I was going through, he'd find some way to turn it around and make it about him, leaving me feeling more isolated than ever.

Releasing the memories has been the hardest thing I have ever dealt with. They were shrouded in pain, guilt, shame, and disbelief. Each one was accompanied by doubt and denial. I wanted to heal from all of this, but that was easier said than done. One step I hoped would help was to talk to my mother about what happened, but that scared me as much as the memories. I'd come to realize that more than likely my mother, as a child, had also been sexually abused by her father. I recognized the rage that swelled up inside of her. It was something I also had to deal with. My hope was that by opening up and discussing my memories with her, we both might receive some healing. I struggled with this. The thought of telling her terrified me. How would she react? Would she believe me? Would she hate me? Maybe she would never want to see or speak to me again. Scenario after scenario went through my mind.

Because I was so afraid to tell her, I convinced myself none of it was true. It was just my craziness coming out, I told myself. These events could not have happened. Just forget it and move on. But the universe had other ideas. Every night I did battle in my dreams. Guns and knives and bombs—my dreams were an all-out war zone. This went on for weeks. Finally, I couldn't stand waking up in a sweat any longer and I proclaimed to the Universe, "All right, you win. I believe it. It did happen." The dream wars ended. I began working up the courage to talk to Mom.

All of this was happening while Glenn and I were going through one of those rough spots. On top of it all, Glenn received a job offer to work in Cincinnati. I debated whether the children and I should even go with him. Our marriage was rocky at best. In fact, I wasn't sure Glenn wanted us to come. I still loved Glenn and it was sad to think about our family breaking up. But on my modest wage at *Aquarius*, even with child support from Glenn, trying to get by on our own would have been tough.

We decided to stick it out and make the move. We'd sold our house and Glenn was already at his new job in Cincinnati when I made the decision to tell Mom about my memories. Our two children and I were staying with my mom and dad while the kids finished the school quarter, so if the talk didn't go well, I didn't know what to expect.

Having my courage worked up, I sat down and told Mom I'd been sexually abused as a child. She was shocked. But when I revealed that it was her father, she was speechless. She told me, "I can't talk about this right now, but we'll talk about it another time." I understood that. It hadn't been easy for me accept, so it wasn't surprising she would need some time to digest it.

Later that night I opened my bedroom door and overheard Mom tell Dad, "I believe that she believes it." I closed the door and let them talk. Over the next few months, I waited patiently for my mother to bring the subject up again, but she never did. Our initial discussion was the first and last time we ever spoke of it.

Having family support would have made the healing easier. I talked to one sister about my memories. I don't know if she believed me, but she was supportive and a good listener. Unfortunately she was my only support. One sibling refused to believe me and another was full of anger upon hearing the accusations. When I told another sibling about the abuse and relayed that I had talked with Mom, they replied, "No wonder Mom has been in such a horrid mood this week." They went on to assure me we had a pretty good childhood and explained how messed up a friend's family was (unlike ours). That was it. Subject closed. My healing would be my own. Family was not going to be a part of it. Maybe I should have pushed more to bring it out in the open years ago, but dealing with it myself was hard enough without having to defend my memories to the family.

Two of my sisters owned an antique and resale shop. Mom would go to garage sales with one of them most every Friday to find merchandise to resell. While she wouldn't talk to me about the abuse, Mom did open up and talk to her about the conversation we had. My sister in turn relayed some of their discussions to me. Some of the memories Mom recalled of her dad reinforced my belief that she was also a victim. She told my sister that, as a child, she would often dance with her dad, until one night he abruptly told her, "You're too old for this," and the dancing stopped.

Grampa also had a controlling personality. I'd already recognized this from stories I grew up with, such as the time my mother mentioned to him that she would be buying bedroom furniture for her girls. He immediately went out and bought the furniture he wanted us to have. But not as a gift. My parents were expected to pay him back, even though it was not at all what my mother had her heart set on. Being the compliant daughter, however, she accepted the furniture.

But I was shocked when she confessed to my sister that she hadn't been sure if she wanted to marry my father. Grampa pushed her into it, telling her he would be a good provider (and he was). I also found out she'd hoped to be a nurse, but my grandfather didn't like the idea. He thought she'd see too much of the world. She ended up getting her degree in a field she didn't want to be in. She was definitely under his control.

I was still hopeful my mother and I would talk someday, but those hopes were dashed when my sister told me about another conversation that took place between the two of them. One day, Mom told her, "I've come to terms with it and I can't believe I ever doubted my father." Dead for years and he still had power over her.

After learning of the abuse, I expected Mom to feel pain, to cry, to be upset, maybe even to scream and shout. I expected her to do something—to show some kind of emotion, good or bad. Instead, she acted as if I'd never told her (in our family we often talked about things behind one another's backs, not face-to-face). I poured my heart out to her and from where I stood, she didn't seem to care. I wanted her to believe me. I needed her support. I wanted her to remember her own childhood. Without her support and belief, I felt victimized and abandoned all over again.

I loved my mom. I tried to understand and accept that she was dealing with it the only way she knew how. We all do the best we can. But knowing that didn't make it any easier to control my feelings. Depending on what stage of healing I was going through, my emotions ranged from love and understanding to acceptance to deep, deep anger. When she was sick and dying, I was angry. Angry that she never acknowledged what happened to me. Angry that I was still struggling with healing, a struggle that would have been so much easier if we could have talked about it.

I understood how hard it was for her. She was a victim too, even if she wouldn't admit it to herself. I could see it in the rages she went into. When she was growing up, it wasn't discussed. She had no one to go to for help. I'd hoped my remembering would help us both. But at some level I guess I was still scared of her angry outbursts. I knew if I brought up the subject again that it would be an ugly scene and she would make life hell for everyone around her. My courage apparently wasn't that strong. I was my mother's child.

CHAPTER 19

The Child In White

THANKS TO A PAST LIFE REGRESSION I gained some important insights into our relationship and I've been able to let go of the anger felt toward my mother. The memory of this past life began unfolding many years ago as I was first starting to do my own healing work.

One day as I lay down to do some release work, the image of a child came into my mind. I'd previously gotten a glimpse of this child named Angel, a sweet girl about four or five years old. As I previously described, she had long dark hair and was wearing a simple, white nightgown-like garment. Angel's arms were wrapped around a doll that looked exactly like her. Sticking out of the doll's chest was a knife and bright red blood was dripping down the front of her gown. At the time I first saw Angel, I had no idea what any of this meant.

Memories had been coming out slowly for me, as if to let me process one part at a time, because seeing the whole picture at once would have been too much to handle. Needing to digest and accept it bit by bit, the images would often come out first in metaphoric form or be symbolic in nature. Already being emotionally distressed, I believe this was a way to let me cope without sending me over the top psychologically.

This time as the images came up, I was given more of the story. The dark-haired little girl was aptly named, looking like an angel in her white gown. Very sweet and innocent. The setting was a little vague but I got the impression she, or we (I was beginning to see that she was me), were in a temple or large open cave of sorts with enormous rock walls. I was placed on a marble-like slab sitting on two upright pillars of stone, such as an altar would be.

My grandfather was there in his robes and a hat that reminded me of the tall bishops' mitres I'd seen as a child. There was a gathering of people in front of the altar. My mother watched from the shadows off to the side. It was over so quickly—my heart had been cut out and my white gown was stained with bright red blood. With this vision I felt nothing of what the child felt, I simply saw what had transpired.

But for myself, I felt shock. I knew instantly I'd lived this life in the past and had been brutally sacrificed at the hands of my grandfather as my mother stood by and did nothing to protect me. I immediately recognized the key players: my grandfather, my mother, and myself. We were all playing the same roles in this life. This was not a pattern I wanted to repeat again, but the hurt of having been unprotected in both lives was not an easy thing for me to let go.

Over the years, I continued to do my healing work. But as hard as I tried, I never totally rid myself of the anger I felt toward my mother for not protecting me in that life, or in this life. I still loved my mother, and, to the world, I played my role as a caring daughter. Inside, my feelings and emotions were all over the place—sometimes angry, sometimes caring and sympathetic, often frustrated that we couldn't talk about our childhoods. Twenty or so years would pass as I dealt with these feelings, but eventually I would find there was unfinished business with that little girl. The whole story hadn't been told.

Sometimes I'd get an uneasiness that seemed to be telling me "there's more work to do." I'd had that feeling for a while and finally decided to address it, inviting a friend to come to my home and lead me in a past life regression.

As I was taken back in time, a past life started to emerge and I muttered, "I've seen this one before." I wondered if I was trying to force something to come out or if I was grabbing at anything I could find. But as the images began to get clearer, they became more real. I could see the child (myself) on the altar and my grandfather (who seemed to be the high priest) and the crowd whose chants were reaching feverish tones.

Just as quick as before, it was over. My heart had been cut out and there was my grandfather holding it high in the air for everyone to see. I'd been sacrificed. But that was not the end of my vision this time.

I found myself in spirit form kneeling in front of my mother as she sat sobbing, obviously in a great deal of pain. I tried to comfort her, to tell her it was okay, that I was fine. But, of course, she could not see me or hear me. Soon I heard the roar from the crowd as it grew louder. I watched as they carried my mother off over their heads. Although I did not see what happened next, I knew she, too, was being sacrificed.

A moment later my mother and I found our spirit selves sitting side by side. We were no longer mother and child but appeared to be about the same adolescent age, perched on rafters high above the scene we'd just left. It was as if the temple setting below us was a stage and my grandfather and the crowd were actors. It felt like watching a play. My mother and I were obviously the best of friends. I turned to her and said, "We'll get it right the next time." We both smiled, completely at peace with the situation. In that moment, our non-physical selves understood that life is about learning and growing. We knew that life is eternal and there would always be another opportunity for the growth we sought. We had no regrets, just love.

Coming out of this session, I could clearly see how this past life paralleled my current life. The controlled grip my grandfather held on my mother left her helpless to defend herself or me. She stood by and let me be sacrificed in that life, just as she stood by in this life and let me be abused by him again, too afraid to stand up to him.

But this was such a healing memory for me. Although I knew relationships changed from life to life and we played various roles, I previously had a hard time seeing my mother as anything but my mother, someone who was supposed to protect me, but didn't.

Now when I think of my mom, I can picture her as a friend and a spiritual soulmate - someone who did the best she could, as we all do. Maybe she still didn't "get it right" this time, but I know her nonphysical self is supporting me and rooting for me to do my best. And I know that in time, when she is ready, she will be able to assert herself. As for me, I feel that I'm finished with this script and ready to move forward.

CHAPTER 20

The Move To Cincinnati

I N DECEMBER, SOON AFTER I HAD the conversation with my mom about my emerging memories, Adam, Alix and I joined Glenn in our new home in Fairfield, a suburb north of Cincinnati. My relationship with Glenn got back on track and things were pretty good for the next few years. Getting away from my family right at that point of my healing process was a good thing. The miles between us gave me more freedom to work on my healing without family judgments.

I'm a big believer in signs and I got confirmation we'd made a good choice in moving the family to Cincinnati. The double kitchen window in our new home looked out over a wide-open, grassy backyard.

Several times during those first few months in our new home, I'd look out the window and see a big, beautiful rainbow that spanned the entire backyard. The universe seemed to be telling me I'd made a good decision. We lived in that house for close to ten years and after those first few months I never saw the rainbows again. Our marriage was fine by then and I didn't need to be reassured.

It wasn't long before I found a skillful group in Fairfield called Partners in Healing. Judy, the hypnotherapist there, held a weekly meeting for incest survivors. This was my first time in a group gathering, but it was small and supportive so I looked forward to these sessions. My private hypnotherapy appointments with Judy were also helpful in bringing out more children and memories.

Judy introduced me to Sheilah, another partner in the group. Sheilah was a massage therapist who also offered a long list of other healing services. My entire life I've had body image issues, so massage was not a consideration for me, but I loved her Reiki sessions — something I'd not experienced before. She was a gifted healer with a great, positive energy about her. I continued the Reiki sessions on a regular basis and occasionally would try one of her other healing services such as reflexology. All the therapy and healing techniques were helping and I worked hard on my own to get past the damage the abuse had caused. Little by little I was healing, but there were still many times when I couldn't see the progress. It seemed to be an endless process.

Financially, I needed to be working. My resume was good and finding a job was not a problem, but trying to keep my emotions under control made me nervous. Mood swings and depression were regular occurrences and I wasn't sure how well I could keep it together. The jobs available to me were nothing more than a paycheck, anyways, and I found little personal satisfaction in them.

My interest in metaphysics and spirituality was continuing to grow. Believing I would be much happier working in that arena, I enrolled in a series of hypnotherapy classes offered in nearby Dayton. The instructors were wonderful and I thoroughly enjoyed everything about these courses. I found camaraderie with several of the other students and for the first time I didn't feel out of place in school.

After completing several levels of course work I received my certificate as a Certified Clinical Hypnotherapist. Judy had temporarily left Partners in Healing by then, leaving an office space open. Not being in the best of financial situations at the time, I was grateful to Sheilah and her partner for working out an arrangement for me and I began seeing clients at Partners in Healing. Although I thought I was ready to work with people as a hypnotherapist and become part of the metaphysical healing community, I soon found out I wasn't. I lacked trust and self-confidence. I didn't trust myself to know what to say and I didn't trust the universe to guide me. In my personal life, I was still dealing with childhood issues, not as in your face as they used to be, but how was I going to help anyone else when I was still struggling?

By this time our financial situation was out of control. We were heavy into credit card debt and living from paycheck to paycheck. Not being able to see a way out, I called my parents sobbing. They may not have known how to support me emotionally, but they were able to give us some financial relief. We put ourselves on a strict budget and I went back to work. Getting ourselves back on track monetarily was a big motivator to me and I was surprisingly successful in my commissioned telemarketing job. Paying off our debt and the loan from my parents was of primary importance.

After a year, we were debt free again (at least for a short time; this was a lesson to be repeated), but by this time I'd lost my motivation and my sales were slipping. I left that job and stayed home for a time. It was nice to be able to refocus on my healing and to take time for long walks in nature. I knew eventually I would need to return to work, but I loved having this time to myself and not being on someone else's schedule.

CHAPTER 21

Life Success

FTER MOVING TO CINCINNATI, GLENN ENTERED into a personal development phase. He was introduced to a program called Life Success. It was a personal growth platform that worked well for him. The four-day "basic" seminars let his voice be heard while interacting with a large group of people that would break out into smaller groups to work on individual issues. He found himself to be someone whom people could turn to for help. He was great at listening to other's problems and expounding his words of wisdom. He enjoyed these weekends and, over the years, repeated the course several times as a small group leader. He later went on to take the advanced program.

The first time he came home from a weekend seminar I was thrilled. It made a deep impact on him. He was more open, more caring and understanding. He was not so quick to judge and seemed to really want to be helpful and supportive of other people. But after a few months he was back to his old ways. The same thing happened each time he repeated the course. Big change, then back to his old self. I'm happy to say that eventually permanent changes and growth did occur, but not without frustrations on my part. As much as people loved to come to him for comfort and sage advice, at home he was lost. He had no clue how to deal with his own family's issues.

Glenn believed in the Life Success program and pushed and pushed for me to go to one of these seminars. Because I was working on my issues in my own ways, I resisted for a long time. Many of the concepts he'd been introduced to were new to him but to me were merely variations of ideas I was already familiar with. He liked being the center of attention and mixing with large groups whereas I was the introvert, much preferring individual sessions or small groups. But I finally broke down and agreed to attend the basic program.

The Thursday and Friday evening sessions were fine. Most of the concepts were familiar to me and in line with my beliefs. We did some trust exercises and I even spoke up and participated—something I was not used to doing. But I'd been emotionally upbeat all week and wanted to get the most out of the class. I wasn't working at the time and a good portion of my days were spent walking, meditating, and practicing positive self-talk. I'd convinced myself I could get through "basic" without getting emotional about my issues, but when I stood up and shared during the trust exercise, I could tell how close to the surface my issues were lying.

At home on Friday night, after Glenn went to bed, the tears flowed. My old issues resurfaced. I thought about a regression I'd done with my energy worker, Flenn. During one powerful session I'd regressed into the womb. My soul was in and out, panicked at the prospect of what I was getting into. My mother was distraught. How was she going to handle another baby? My thoughts turned to the time she threw me over the stair railing and my tears came faster and harder.

The tears felt like tears of grief. Grief for what could have been, for who I might have been. Grief for the loss of innocence and for the children that still hurt. I wondered if I would ever really get through it. I'd dealt with these issues so many times before, each time believing I was over them. I comforted myself with the thought that at least I'd shared with others and taken another step in my growth and healing process.

The Saturday sessions went all right. At home I reflected on what I'd learned and realized I was afraid to "want." If I didn't want anything, I wouldn't be disappointed when I didn't get it. But how was anything supposed to come to me if I didn't put out the desire for it? This definitely was not following the Law of Attraction ideals I studied. I needed to deal with all the feelings of worthlessness, of not deserving, fear, shame, guilt. . . . I needed to build myself up and believe in myself. Yet years of negative thoughts were not going away overnight. Telling myself it was important to be patient with my healing process, I was determined to keep working on the positive affirmations and thoughts, and work on emotional issues when they came up, but not dwell on them. The past was over. It was time for me to live in the now and dream for my future.

Reflecting on the Saturday night session in which we'd played a game that divided the group into teams, I had watched as my fellow team members strategized on how to win. There was a lot of discussion and some pretty strong opinions on the best way to play the game. Knowing they were missing the whole point of the exercise (life is not a competition; we are here to support one another), I sat on the sidelines, said nothing, and didn't get involved. By not speaking up and letting my team go down the wrong path, I'd missed some other important aspects of the game, like participating, making myself heard, and helping one another.

Sunday was the last day of the "basic" program and I was feeling great—happy, strong, powerful, and confident. Then the celebration commenced. This was the day to have fun, to celebrate the learning and growth of the past three days. Lively music started playing and people began dancing—looping arms and swinging each other around, going from one partner to the next. It was impossible not to participate. People kept coming up, grabbing me by the arm, and swinging me around. Terror shot through me. I wanted so badly to flee. I wanted to leave and never come back. I didn't belong there. What was I doing here with these people who were having such a good time? Voices in my head were screaming, "Let me out! This is not for me."

How could so many people be enjoying this? Were they truly having a good time? Looking at the seminar leader I saw pure joy on her face. Standing on the outer edge of the group, I tried to force a smile and do my best to fake being involved. Inside I was panicked. I just wanted it to stop. I wanted out.

At lunch, I tried without much success to compose myself. My small group leader knew something was up. She looked at me bewildered and said, "What happened to you? Where did you go (emotionally)?" My face went cold and blank. I was lost somewhere inside. I broke down and ran outside. I didn't go back in for the final afternoon session.

I didn't know where this was coming from. I knew I wasn't the life of the party and had issues with having fun. I never really let myself go. I usually didn't join in. My weight made me self-conscious, but this was not about weight. It was something deeper. It was as if a frozen child all out panicked and took complete control over me. Something had been triggered and whatever it was, it was getting too close to the surface.

I sat outside on a hill near the parking lot, crying. This could be a major roadblock for me. I could choose to either move through it or let it hold me back. It felt like when I made the decision to drop out of college. Not being able to get through the English courses that might reveal too much buried information, I quit altogether. How different might my life have been if I'd managed to somehow get through? Was this also going to hold me back? I wanted to move through it, but hard as I tried I couldn't force myself to go back inside.

Over the next few weeks I worked with my hypnotherapist and tried to find the answers. Why was this child so freaked out about having fun? A few more memories of abuse by my grandfather came up, although not as strong as the earlier ones, and I did gain some clarity. The memory fragments seemed to come from a later time in my childhood than the earlier memories. Someone deeply impressed upon this child that she was not allowed to have fun and she, I, took it to heart and withdrew even further into myself. Again, a child was frozen in time.

It's not that I don't have a sense of humor or don't enjoy having fun, it just has never come easily to me. I observe life from the sidelines—watching, evaluating, wondering how people find it so easy to freely reveal themselves to the world, often envying them for being able to laugh and party and have a good time. I'm more at ease staying in the shadows, not joining in with the partying, dancing, conversations, or laughter. I'll loosen up a bit when I really get to know the people around me, but predominately I'm reserved. I just have a need to feel safe, to truly trust someone before I can relax and be myself around them.

This panic attack triggered the last repressed memories to be revealed. It not only brought up my issues with having fun, but it gave me a clue as to how long the sexual abuse went on. I don't know exactly when it stopped. My guess would be when I was around nine or ten. At ten my breasts were developing and I was probably getting too old for my grandfather. From the story I heard, it sounded like this may have been the same age as my mother was when he stopped dancing with her. At ten years old I was also in the fifth grade. Still quiet and shy, I'd stopped crying at the drop of a hat and could answer the teacher in a voice that, while still soft, at least could be heard. I don't know if the changes had anything to do with the abuse stopping or if it was just part of growing up.

My healing work continued. When first embarking on this journey, I was told it would be like peeling the layers of an onion. I just didn't realize how many layers an onion had.

CHAPTER 22

Depression

I'VE READ THAT WOMEN WHO ARE sexually abused as children are more than twice as likely to suffer from depression than women who have not been abused. Depression has been my companion off and on for most of my life. I've always been known for being moody and there were times as a child I felt withdrawn and retreated to my safe inner world, but I don't recall a bout of depression until I was around twenty.

When I decided to go back to college, I also moved back in with my parents to make school financially feasible. Everything was fine for a while, and I don't know specifically when it originated, but I can remember walking the halls at school, deeply depressed and sure that everyone could see my suffering and pain. Maybe I was just hoping someone would see my agony. I wanted help—relief—but I didn't know how to ask for it.

During this time, Pam called me. She'd been to a psychic for a reading and was told a friend was experiencing depression. It was true, I was depressed. This was probably the first time I'd ever put the word together with the way I was feeling.

Throughout the years, after that first bout when I was barely twenty, the depression came and went. During these gloomy periods I would feel there was no hope for my life to get better. I felt alone, confused, and worthless. There was an intense pain deep inside of me that I didn't understand. My thoughts would often turn to suicide. One way or another, I managed to find a way through each occurrence and continue on.

Although I didn't experience true depression until I was twenty, thoughts of suicide came earlier. There was an episode when I was a senior in high school. At the time, my drug of choice was barbiturates. Sleeping through life was easier than living it. One night I came home from a strange date. For some reason we'd ended up at the cemetery, and as I wandered through I felt calm and peaceful. At home that night, preparing to go to bed, I stood staring into my bathroom mirror for a long time before taking a handful of barbiturates. I'm not sure if I was actually trying to kill myself or if I was hoping someone would see my pain and reach out to help me. I slept for two days without surfacing for meals or leaving my room for any reason. My bedroom was in the lower level of the house and my parents were busy with work, household chores, and my two younger brothers who were still active in sports and school activities. No one noticed the absence of the teenager sleeping in the basement bedroom.

I wasn't keeping journals so I don't remember how often the depression was coming as an adult, but I do vividly remember an incident that happened during one of these periods of despair. I was in my mid-thirties at the time and journaled about it later:

MAD, MAD ANGEL

I had one especially bad episode of depression that ended in a way I'll never forget. I was in an awful state. The hopelessness I felt was deeper than any I'd ever experienced up until that point. There was no way out. I'd had enough.

The pain was so unfathomable I could not work my way through it this time. It was time to end it. I came to that conclusion as tears rolled down my face. I thought about my two young children, but I was sure they would be better off without me and my emotional ups and downs. Pounding on the steering wheel of my car, I shouted angrily to God and let him know how much I hated him and life. I'd thought about it before, but I was actually going to do it this time. I was ready to end my life.

I remember precisely where I was when I made the decision. Driving down a busy road, I was headed south and stopped in traffic. Still in an awful state, something caught my eye and I looked to my left at the passing car headed north. The driver looked identical to the MAD magazine character Alfred E. Neuman. I don't mean similar, I mean EXACTLY, like this person had a cartoon character for a head. He was looking directly at me, leaning out his window, holding a wand and blowing bubbles toward me. Despite my state of mind, I couldn't help but laugh at this comical sight. It was instantaneous. The dark cloud I had been under lifted off me immediately.

Angels come to us in many forms and I will never believe my bubble blowing savior was anything but an angel sent to rescue me from myself.

Life continued on with my mood swings and bouts of depression. The mood swings I associated more with my hellish monthly cycle. The number of bad emotional days each month seemed to grow as the years went on. This was when my rage would reach its peak. Feeling absolutely out of control, I'd scream and yell, slam doors, then use every bit of the power I could muster not to smash mirrors and windows. If he was around, my poor husband took the brunt of these outbursts. I shouted awful things at him and blamed him for all my problems. I'm not sure I would have stayed if our roles had been reversed.

I tried going on various anti-depressants but did not find one that worked well for me. Prozac was the first one prescribed. During my short time on Prozac, peculiar thoughts would come up. Several times I found myself standing in the kitchen with a knife in my hand and contemplating what I could do with it (bodily harm to me or others). In other instances, we'd be driving down the highway and the thought would go through my mind, "I could just open this door and jump out." I went off the medication because I didn't like the way I felt on it, but the scary thing was, I didn't realize how strange and dangerous these thoughts were until I stopped taking the pills.

With the next medication I tried, my head seemed as if it were encased in a cloud. Life appeared to be unreal. There were strong emotions inside of me, but they felt as if they were stuck at chest level. I just couldn't get them out.

A third medication zapped me of all motivation. At work I'd just sit at my desk staring out the window. While on a business trip to San

Francisco, one of my favorite cities to visit, its charm was wasted on me because of this medication. When my group had some free time for sightseeing, I told them to go on without me and took a cab back to the hotel to do nothing.

That was the end of taking anti-depressants for several years. Of course, I'd gone through mainstream medicine to get my medications. Each time the doctor would ask what was going on. When I would tell them about dealing with childhood sexual abuse, the first thing out of their mouth would be "false memory syndrome". (It always amazed me that they could make this diagnosis after listening to me talk for less than five minutes, not really knowing anything about me or my life.) But they were more than happy to prescribe medication. Most of the time they never followed up to see how I was doing, even at my next visit.

False Memory Syndrome. I wanted to explode every time I heard these words. The pain I felt wasn't coming from some suggestion by a therapist. The emotions I experienced didn't come from any stories I had made up. Why would I make them up? I didn't want to be in therapy, I didn't want to be suicidal, I didn't want to break down without a moment's notice. Who would put themselves through the unbearable emotional pain and rage I felt? Yes, anger flared up inside me every time I heard the words. I've read the reports, I know the explanations. On any subject, you can pick a side and make a convincing argument for or against it. Recovering from false memory syndrome would have been easier than recovering from the truth. I didn't want these memories to be true, but each time I tried to deny them, the mental and emotional turmoil got worse.

At one point, I decided to try mainstream therapy and made an appointment with a psychiatrist. Looking down, shaking her head, she laughed to herself as I told my story and again I heard the words "false memory syndrome." I vowed that would be the last time I mentioned the abuse to the medical community.

Many years later, while going through menopause, the depression was almost constant. I'd force myself to go to work and put on a good face, but when I got home I'd shut myself away in my office feeling sad and lonely, hopeless and in despair. I'd cry for hours at a time. The pain felt so deep, it was unimaginable that it could get any worse.

Journaling helped me unleash a lot of anger, but something else was also happening. After each session of uncontrollable crying and angry journaling, I'd start automatic writing. I didn't know where this was coming from—angels, guides, my higher self, or maybe my own inner knowing. Whatever it was, it was full of love and wisdom.

Journal Entry:

> *I feel so lost. I am so tired of fighting the depression. I don't want to do anything. There is no motivation. I just want to hide out in my own little world. I feel empty, uninspired, useless, worthless. I have no passion in life or for life. I'm tired of fighting it. I'm tired of trying. I want to give up. The moods change so quickly. I've tried to fight it. That works for a while, but it always comes back.*

Channeled Writing:

> *Love yourself as we love you. Know you are precious to us. Know we will always be there to support you. You must learn to support yourself. You are so special, so courageous. We know it is a struggle for you. We understand your fears, your doubts. You must give in and trust the process. Stop fighting it. Just allow. Allow All-That-Is to take charge of your life, to support you in times of need. Do not be afraid to give up control. Control is what is holding you back. Take a chance. Believe in the power of the universe to give you the life you want. Let go. Free yourself to believe.*

Give up control and trust. Know you are good. Let the universe take over. Let the universe work its magic. Relax and enjoy. Let go of the need for perfection. You are perfection just as you are.

These automatic writing sessions gave me temporary emotional relief. Still, suicidal thoughts were my constant companion. Almost a crutch. When something went wrong it was the first thought to come to me. I'd tell myself, "if it gets too bad, I can always kill myself." Even if this wasn't a serious consideration, it was there. I began to look forward to the tears and the relief they would bring. The deep, deep pain was so familiar it somehow felt comfortable, but at the same time unbearable. As a last resort, to get through this period of my life, I decided to try anti-depressants again.

I felt as though I had no alternative. If I wanted to live, I needed help. I wanted to live for my children. Envisioning how ending my life would affect them often made me continue on. Would they feel responsible? Would they ask themselves if they could have prevented it? No, I didn't want them to have the emotional baggage I'd carried around all my life. The other thing that kept suicide at bay was my spiritual beliefs. Although I didn't believe I would be punished for committing suicide, I did believe it would affect my spiritual evolution. If I didn't find my way through the problems in this life, I feared I would be doomed to repeat the experience in another life. I was working so hard to heal, I didn't want to have to deal with all of this again.

In some ways, the newer medication worked better for me. There was relief from the deep pain and despair, but I still wasn't where I wanted to be emotionally. A second medication was added. This helped, but the most I ever felt was being "even" with rare moments of feeling happy for no reason. I pictured my emotions in relationship to a graph. Without the meds I was often way, way below the center line, at the bottom of the graph. With the meds, I was mostly even with the center line. Would I ever be able to feel true joy? I so wanted that graph line to go as high above the center line as it'd been below the line.

With the medications there were also side effects. Physical side effects included loss of balance, loss of sexual desire, leg jerking at night, and ringing in my ears. I didn't sleep well, lacked energy, words didn't always come out right, and my memory seemed to be affected, among other things. One of the worst side effects for me was that I was having difficulty remembering my dreams, and my lucid dreams that I looked forward to were gone. It was hard to stay focused and often difficult to hear my angels and guides, which also made it more difficult to do my automatic writing. Excessive shopping and making poor decisions also seemed to be side effects.

My last serious consideration of suicide came after a fantastic vacation and while I was still on the medications, although I admit I did miss a few doses while on our trip. We'd been to the Caribbean and, as a result of my medication induced poor decision making, let ourselves get caught up in a scam. At the time, Glenn simply wanted me to be happy, so he went along with whatever I wanted. It wasn't until we got back home that we realized we'd been scammed out of five thousand dollars. Anxiety struck. I was a wreck for a week. I lost six pounds because I couldn't eat and I couldn't sleep. I spent a lot of time pacing and spelling out words in my head (this is now a sign for me that I am anxious). It felt like my life was over, an irrational thought to have because of five thousand dollars. We'd been in far worse debt than that before. By the end of the week I was crying hysterically and couldn't stop. Thoughts of suicide would not go away. Glenn didn't know how bad it had gotten and was frustrated with trying to reason with me. He couldn't deal with it anymore, and one morning left the house in anger. Things got worse. My thoughts were getting more and more irrational and depressive. Suicide was the only solution I could think of. I didn't know what to do. I needed help. I called my sister, but she was downtown and could not get to me soon, so I asked her to call Glenn. He came right home in a panic, afraid of what he might find, because when I got in these states of depression or anxiety I often proclaimed my wish to be dead.

This resulted in a trip to the emergency room. Still crying uncontrollably, the nurse could see I was in a bad way and immediately showed me to a small room. The doctor came in quickly to check on me. The nurse soon instructed me to undress completely and put on a hospital gown. My clothes were taken out of the room. I was taken to another, more open, examination room. Glenn observed the nurses coming in every couple of minutes to check on me and then remove, item by item, anything I could use to harm myself.

After a few hours, the crying stopped and I calmed down as always happens following an episode of releasing. The doctor was supportive and asked if I had a history of being abused. We talked about what triggered this episode and about my past. There were no references to false memory syndrome this time. Glenn later told me that when the subject of the abuse came up, my whole face and body changed. He said he hadn't realized how much it still affected me.

Going to a treatment center would not be covered by my insurance plan and would be extremely expensive. By this time, I was pretty well calmed down and we agreed being admitted to any institution would add to my anxiety, so the doctor released me with the name of a psychiatrist to see and the promise I would be more careful not to miss any doses of my medication.

The psychiatrist added a new medication, explained that she only treated the medical side of depression, and referred me to therapy. The meds were working well enough that it was difficult to express the great pain I was in when the depression was at its peak. I didn't connect emotionally with the therapist who'd been recommended and didn't go back again for a second appointment. I gained ten pounds in the first month on the new pills. The extra weight was not helping my mood, so I returned to just my old medications and continued on.

Through working with a hypnotherapist a couple years later, I was finally able to understand why I'd had such a severe reaction to being scammed. Someone took something from me without my permission. I equated it with the abuse. In both instances I felt victimized, as though I had no control over what happened to me. As survivors often do, I felt the need to be in control. My control issues played out in my relationships, my jobs, and other ways I hadn't even realized up until that point.

As I continued my hypnotherapy sessions I was getting to a better place emotionally. Eventually, I tired of the side effects from the antidepressants and discontinued one of my medications. A few months later I dropped the other medication and now have been off antidepressants for several years. I was learning and understanding more and more about the power that comes from controlling thoughts and therefore emotions. I'd been hearing the words for a long time, but not fully comprehending them. Now I was beginning to put into action the wisdom I was hearing—learning to catch the negative thoughts early and stop them. Not always an easy thing to do, but with practice my ability to control my thoughts was improving. At the least, I could turn them around more quickly. Periods between depressive episodes were stretching out. When I did get depressed, I was able to bring myself out much quicker. Instead of depression lasting for weeks or months, it was now a matter of only a couple of days and, as time went on, usually just hours.

I embraced Abraham's teaching that my emotions are a result of my thoughts and an indicator of how aligned I am with my higher self. I understood now that my higher self is always in a state of love and joy. The more joyful I am, the more closely aligned I am with my higher self. Any time I'm feeling a negative emotion, I'm out of alignment. My work is to find my way back into alignment. Life is definitely easier when I stay aligned.

Negative feelings and depression-like episodes have become less and less common for me but they still do occur on occasion. By paying attention to my emotions, I can typically catch myself and keep my thoughts from gathering momentum and going downhill. Sometimes it's as easy as telling myself, "You're not going there today." Other times I have to pull out my "tool box" (tips, tricks, and techniques that I have collected over the years to guide me to a better-feeling place) and work on getting my thoughts turned around.

There are still times when I'm just not ready to let go of the negative thoughts, or I simply ignore them and let the negativity take hold. Once the despondent feelings start up, it takes more effort to get back to a good place. As I was writing this book I let this happen. I tried several times to get back to a good place but would quickly get disturbed again. From past experience, I knew that after a good cry I was going to feel emotional relief and be able to move forward once more. I forced myself to focus on even more negative thoughts and, as usual, the tears came pouring out. After my cry and some journaling, I felt much better, but also a little guilty that I was doing this on purpose. Maybe, I thought, I should have tried harder to focus on the positive.

To gain some clarity, I meditated on the strategy I had used. Immediately, they (my guides) showed me a sling shot being pulled back and an object being propelled forward. They said that yes, I was taking a step backwards with the negative thinking, but the result was that I was pushed forward further and more quickly than I would have been without the emotional release. At times, this is my best and quickest defense, but it's not something I would suggest to most people. Before I learned the power of my thoughts and how to control them they could have sunk me into a long depressive episode. I am at a point now where I can go there and bring myself back. I no longer fear getting stuck.

Note: I would never advise anyone to avoid depression medication or to get off the medication they are on. At the time I started taking anti-depressants I was desperate and I do believe they helped me through some rough periods of my life. What I would encourage anyone dealing with depression to do is to not coast while on the medication. Either on your own or with a therapist, do the inner work you need to do in order to heal. It can be hard work and your wounds probably won't heal overnight, but you can gradually find relief and hopefully, in time, you will be able to lessen or go off your meds.

CHAPTER 23

Self-Esteem

ABUSE SURVIVORS TYPICALLY HAVE LOW SELF-ESTEEM. I was no exception, never feeling worthy or good enough. I was painfully shy and quiet. I stuffed my feelings with food and felt ashamed of my body—a pattern that began in childhood and a problem that I still struggle with today. Looking back now, I see a child that was crying out for help and no one heard her. By the time third grade rolled around, I wouldn't speak above a whisper in class and cried if the teacher or an adult reprimanded me in any way. I can remember one day, near the end of a catechism class, I was cold in that damp basement and pulled on the coat hanging on the back of my chair. The priest, sure I was trying to get ready to go early, yelled at me and said it wasn't time to go yet. I bit my lip, but said nothing to defend my actions. Then I heard one of my classmates whisper to her friend, "Watch, she's going to cry." I fought back the tears the best I could.

Fourth grade wasn't any better. I was still talking in whispers and sensitive to any criticism, crying if someone even looked at me wrong. At recess, I watched while the other kids played, but rarely joined in. Writing assignments were my worst nightmare, and there seemed to be lots of them that year. The most horrifying part for me was that the teacher read them aloud to the class and critiqued them. Often, I never turned them in. When I did turn in a writing assignment, I would feign a stomachache and stay home the day she was to read them. If I miscalculated and she read my story when I was there, I wanted to crawl under my desk and disappear.

It wasn't until long after I released the memories that I understood why I was so afraid of having my stories read. It was letting someone see inside of me, giving them a glimpse of who I was, and the possibility they would see the precious secrets I'd so carefully stowed away.

Fourth grade was also the year of my most humiliating event. My body and bodily functions were shameful to me. In physical education class, we were supposed to wash up in a large group shower area before getting dressed and returning to class. This wasn't something I could do. My mother had to write a note asking for me to be excused. Even using the bathrooms at school was hard for me. I had a shy bladder and if there were others in the girls room, I often couldn't go. On one of these occasions I went back to class not having been able to relieve myself. By late in the day I needed to go badly, but it was only ten minutes until school was out. Being timid, I was afraid to ask the teacher to let me be excused, sure she would say no, explaining that it was almost time to go home and for me to wait. I tried hard to hold it, but about five minutes before the bell rang my bladder said "enough," and sitting at my desk, surrounded by the whole class, out it came. I was embarrassed beyond belief. Humiliated. How could I ever show my face again? Faking sickness the next day, I had the weekend to recover. Before this writing I have never discussed this with anyone. Not even my husband. This natural bodily function was so shameful to me.

In fifth grade, I was still very shy and quiet but I think this was around the time the sexual abuse stopped. Things were getting a little better, but I continued to have a difficult time with creative writing throughout my school days. In fact, in high school I flunked English because I simply would not turn in any writing assignments. I dropped out of college when I realized there was no way I could get through the mandatory English classes and their writing exercises. At the time, things were still buried deep inside and my inner child guards were not about to let anyone in or anything out.

I wonder now how no one saw the pain I was in. This child seemed to be crying out for help even though she could not express it in words. I would hope in today's more educated society someone would recognize the signs and come to the aid of a child in such deep trouble, but I know too many wounded children still go unnoticed. I look back at my own children and ask myself if I was there for them. Did I notice when they needed help? How often do we not see children who are in anguish?

Self-esteem is still an issue I struggle with today. At times, I doubt my ability and my worth. I'm sometimes sure no one likes or cares about me, that I am not worthy of their time or trouble.

CHAPTER 24

Learning To Love Myself

THE YEARS THAT FOLLOWED THE INITIAL remembering and therapy were filled with ups and downs, periods of spiritual growth and long periods of feeling stuck. It definitely wasn't like in the movies or books where someone has a breakthrough and lives happily ever after. Reading that type of story didn't instill me with hope, but rather a sense of failure and frustration. I'd ask myself, "What's wrong with me? Why can't I heal?" The memories had been released, so why couldn't I just put it all behind me?

I came to understand that it is not just letting go of the abusive acts I'd lived through. What happened shaped who I was and had molded me into this person I'd become. I had no boundaries. Personal boundaries are normally formed early in childhood, but with my abuse starting as an infant, I had no opportunity to establish healthy barriers. I didn't know how to protect myself—mentally, physically, or emotionally. I didn't know how to say no or how to stand up for myself. I was filled with shame, doubt, and guilt. I didn't know how to respect myself or take responsibility for my actions. I blamed others for my condition, for the failures in my life, and for the intense inner pain that at times seemed to be my constant companion. I wanted the world to see my pain. I wanted the world to join me in my pain, a pain I was still hiding deep inside, only allowing a select few to get a glimpse of what I was going through.

Counseling taught me that I needed to learn to love myself. But I didn't have a clue what that meant. I was trying, coming up with countless ways to help myself heal—pages of positive affirmations, a notebook with ideas to bring me out of my depressions, journaling, anger release work, and on and on. Each of these things were helping me to heal, but it was a long, slow process and the evidence of healing was often hard or impossible for me to see. Through it all, the real meaning of loving myself still was not clear to me.

It's only been in the last couple of years that I have begun to grasp the concept of what loving myself truly means. Through Abraham's teachings I have learned we all have a non-physical part—our inner being (some call it our soul or higher self). While I have been aware of this for a long time, it wasn't until I truly understood that this part of us stays in a state of joy at all times—always seeing us with love and appreciation, never judging us—that I began to understand how to love myself. When I'm down on myself, I often must remind myself of how the universe feels about me, about every one of us. We are loved unconditionally. Always. No matter what.

I know there is still work to do to truly love all of me. But I do have a better understanding now of what it means to love myself. I know that part of loving myself is letting go of these feelings and beliefs. I catch myself in negative self-talk and try to be aware enough to turn it around and be kinder and more loving to myself.

These are some of the things I now strive to remember and practice:

- I am a beautiful spiritual being.
- The Universe loves and adores me just the way I am.
- I treat myself with love, kindness, respect, and appreciation.
- I trust myself and the Universe.
- I love myself as I am right now.
- I forgive myself and others.
- Tending to my spiritual needs, like meditating, is important.
- I align with my higher self.
- I look for the good in myself and everyone around me.
- I praise myself often and accept praise from others.
- It benefits me to focus on my strengths and let go of comparisons.
- I practice gratitude and appreciation.
- I live in the present moment.
- It benefits me to care for my body by exercising and eating right.
- I talk kindly and respectfully to myself and about myself.
- I focus my thoughts and pay attention to my feelings.
- I believe in myself and do what I love.
- I love myself, so I let go of doubts and fears.
- I accept love from others and embrace it.
- Loving myself means telling myself "I love you," every day.
- I seek and choose joy.

I often remind myself "Nothing is more important than that I feel good." (This is my favorite Abraham quote and it means not having to be right, letting go of anger and jealousy, and not holding onto anything that does not feel good.)

When I am not sure how to love myself, I focus on what my inner being would do or say or how my inner being would act or feel, and then I do my best to emulate it.

Learning to love myself is a process. It takes practice. I'm working on it.

CHAPTER 25

Return To Atlanta

WE'D BEEN IN CINCINNATI FOR ALMOST ten years when one summer we visited Atlanta, a trip that would change the direction of our lives. While chatting with my sisters, we conveyed Glenn's dissatisfaction with his job. Internal problems, stress between the husband and wife owners, and lack of the financial compensation and the personal recognition he deserved were taking its toll. The stress was getting to him and he was ready for a change. I was only working part-time and had no real attachment to my job.

As they caught us up on how well their antique and resale shop was doing, my sisters, half joking, said they would find us a space if we were interested. My younger sister owned a five-bedroom home that she lived in with her two high school age daughters, the oldest being a few months younger than my youngest. She threw out an offer to let us stay with them while we got our new business underway. We didn't seriously consider the proposal until the topic came up on our drive back to Cincinnati.

Doing things on a whim was new for me. But as I was healing and getting older I was letting go of some of my control issues. I'd always been a careful planner, to the point that even our vacation itineraries would be printed out in detail. But that was beginning to change. The first time I noticed this was when my husband mentioned looking at new cars. I had no intention of buying anything, but I found a car I liked and bought it on the spur of the moment.

Moving back to Atlanta was another impulsive action, but the timing seemed right. Adam was in college and away from home. Alix was going to be a senior in high school, but most of her friends had recently graduated and would be away at college so leaving them was not an issue. She was also coming out as being openly gay, so this would give her a fresh start where she could be herself.

I called my sister to see if she was serious about us moving in with her. She was. The decision was made quickly. Schools in Georgia are back in session by early August and we wanted Alix to be there at the start of her senior year. We got the house ready to go on the market and Alix and I headed back to Georgia while Glenn stayed in Fairfield until the house sold, which was fairly quickly. He was able to join us as soon as he wrapped things up at his job.

My sister took me under her wing and we went to garage sales together every Friday and Saturday to search for merchandise. It didn't take long to get the hang of it as I'd been seeking out garage sales since I was a teenager. Although we weren't getting rich, we were making decent profits right away. Working together was going to be a new thing for Glenn and me, and we had our moments, but for the most part we got along fine. Twelve and fourteen or more hour days were not uncommon, but we were enthusiastic about this new life and determined to make a go of it. We'd both had our fill of working for other people. We stayed at the shop for almost fifteen years, the first couple of years as dealers, eventually joining my sisters as owners.

At first, being new to the business, learning the ropes, and working long hours occupied most of my time and the depression seemed to ease up for a period. Focusing on making the business a success took my attention off the past. I was also learning to put the Law of Attraction into action. I found that when I was out of alignment, my sales would slow and inventory would become scarce. However, if I took the time to set my vibration right, furniture and other items for the shop would come in abundance. In fact, sometimes I had to be careful what I asked for. One day when my booth was in need of merchandise, I begged the universe to send me some "big" furniture to restock with. That day we came back to the shop with a giant "Edith Ann" sized chair. After that I was careful to be more specific.

I learned a lot about myself and about how I related to other people during our time at the shop. My need to control became evident. Being a perfectionist Virgo, I wanted everything to be done just right. It was hard for me to understand how others could be satisfied with mediocrity. My best efforts to be organized and have the shop run smoothly were not always appreciated by my co-workers. While I worked hard, I watched others sit and chat the day away. My inability to make others conform to my standards was frustrating to me, to say the least.

But I was beginning to understand we each have our own agendas and I could not force mine on anyone else. I finally concluded that no matter how hard I tried I was not going to change the way anyone else worked or didn't work. Pushing to do so, even in the spirit of improving the business and making everyone more successful, wasn't going to make it happen. My goals were not their goals. All it was doing was wearing me out and keeping me stressed, a stress I put upon myself. As I grew and changed spiritually I liberated myself from the need to be in control. Trying to be in command of things I had no power over was driving me crazy. With the changes that were happening on the inside, I no longer wanted to be the one telling anyone else what they should or should not be doing. That was for them to determine on their own.

It was time to change things up. With the loss of enthusiasm, drive, and determination for the work I had cherished for so many years, I was ready to give the ownership responsibility up and become solely a dealer, as I had been when first starting out at the shop.

CHAPTER 26

Reiki

YEARS AGO, WHILE LIVING IN OHIO, my Reiki sessions with Sheilah were something I always looked forward to. She gave me my first attunement for Reiki I and years later, back in Atlanta, my interest in Reiki was rekindled. I got my certification as a Usui Holy Fire Reiki Level I and Level II practitioner. Reiki means "spiritually guided life energy." It is a healing technique that can be done hands on or hands over the body. This universal healing energy can even be done long distance. It is passed on from one practitioner to another by way of attunements.

Guided meditations were one of my first introductions to metaphysics and I've found them to be extremely helpful throughout my years of doing personal healing work. Whether they are scripted, off-the-cuff, or recorded, I've often had a strong sense of being guided in the visions I see. At times I've seen or spoken with angels or spirit guides during these meditations. The images I'm shown and messages I've received have had a real impact on my life. The Reiki training included several guided meditations. With music playing softly in the background, the instructor guided us through the introduction and then gave us time to finish the first meditation on our own:

> *I am looking across a valley toward some beautiful mountains in the distance. I transform into an eagle and fly to the top of a nearby tree. As I look around, I'm not sure where I should go or what I should be seeing or feeling. I fly to the top of one of the mountains and transform back into human form again. I lay my body down in a grassy field.*

> *I'm surrounded now by a circle of angels. They lift my spirit out of my body and take me to the edge of the mountain. I turn to look behind me and I am saddened to see the great river of tears I have left behind. But looking forward, I can see that the river runs into an ocean. Although I can't see clearly what is in front of me, I know it is beautiful.*

> *Now back in the field again, the angels lead me to and through a large group of people. All eyes are on me, gazing at me with respect and gratitude. I realize these are the people whose lives I can touch. I am led to a beautiful throne-like chair where I can look into the crowd and see everyone.*

That meditation was exceptionally emotional and powerful for me. Many times I have asked myself how one person could have so many tears inside. It was good to receive a message that the tears would lead to something beautiful. It gave me hope for the future. The message reminded me that when I allow love to flow freely, it reaches out and touches so many more. Love is contagious. The more I allow my love to touch others, the more it grows, touching those that come in contact with those whom I have touched. It reaches out endlessly, spreading like wild fire.

In the second meditation, I simply felt energy spinning between my hands for a few minutes. Toward the end it felt as if other hands were on top of mine. I also received this message during the attunement process: Believe in Yourself. Believe Beyond Yourself.

The following year, I took the advanced Reiki training and received my certification for the Usui Holy Fire Reiki ART/Master level. Meditations were again part of this class. I find that every meditation is different, some being nice and relaxing and others being powerful and emotional:

> *In the first meditation, I am standing next to a river. The images are very subtle, more like impressions or an out of focus movie. A group of light beings are on the other side of the river. Two of them cross over and put a gold hooded cloak on me. One being puts their hand on my heart. Things start breaking away from it. I can feel the resistance and walls as they crumble. Doves fly out of my heart. I cross over the river and am lifted up.*

Non-physical entities are assisting me. Again, a nice message of hope for me and assurance that I am not alone. In the next meditation, rainbow stairs are coming out of the clouds. A hand reaches down for me. I take it and climb the stairs. In some meditations, the images are harder to see and it doesn't feel like much is happening. I like to imagine some kind of healing is going on behind the scenes.

The third meditation was again vastly different than the previous ones. The message didn't have the same emotional impact on me, but did give me something to mull over:

> *I am in a glass box. I need to find a way out. There is a small door at the bottom.*

> *I find myself in my childhood yard, walking with a guide and talking. Another guide comes along and takes my hand. There are piles of shit all over the yard. They show me how I can transform the piles of shit into something beautiful. I can do it one by one, or I can blow them all away at one time.*

> *Next, I am on a swing, going very high, flying over trees, flying over the ocean.*

> *Now I find myself sitting, dangling my legs in a pool and talking to my guides. They tell me it is my choice, that I have more power than I believe.*

I saw that everything I considered bad that had happened to me could be turned into something positive and beautiful. It was my choice on how I wanted to do it and how long it would take. The power was mine. I just had to believe it and claim it.

The final meditation triggered some strong emotions from me:

> *Three ETs come to me. They hold up a mirror and I see my reflection, not as I am now, but as an ET. As I see this*

beautiful being of light—my true self—I am close to tears. Then my outer body slips away and inside is my ET body.

I ask why I am here (purpose of my life), and they say I am here as "a light holder."

I ask why I had to go through so much darkness and they say it made my light stronger.

I ask if I was supposed to be a healer (I have been told this several times) and they say I was supposed to seek joy in whatever way made me joyful.

I ask about communicating with them again and they say their messages come to me through Abraham (I suppose that is why I feel so connected to Abraham.)

Next they show me a cobblestone path and the steps in front of me keep lighting up one by one. As I take one step, the next step lights up.

The scene changes and my four-year-old granddaughter comes up and gives me a huge hug. She takes me by the hand and leads me to the top of the earth. We look out on the universe and she points up and says, "That's where we're from."

We talk some. I tell her I miss her. She says I come to see her when she's sleeping. She tells me "sometimes we go home" and sometimes she's the adult and teacher and sometimes I'm the teacher.

I question her about Mama and Pari. Were they ETs too? She just shrugs.

This meditation reminded me that I am on a wonderful path and I need to trust it. I needed to give up some control about how every little thing would happen. If I stayed in alignment and trusted, my path would reveal itself to me, one step at a time. I needed to appreciate and cherish each step as I went along, loving where I was and feeling eager anticipation, not longing, for the next step.

CHAPTER 27

Fear And Trust

F Forgetting
E Everything is
A All
R Right

AFTER BEING IN THE ANTIQUES AND resale business for almost fifteen years, my interest in the shop and the pursuit of inventory to fill my space was waning. Buying, selling, and displaying merchandise had been my top priority. Since giving up ownership, I'd been trying to find balance between work and spiritual growth. But even with less responsibility, work won out too often.

A year after giving up our ownership, Glenn and I finally made the decision to leave the shop entirely. We each had other interests to pursue. Glenn had started portraying Santa Claus a few years before and wanted to spend more time in that pursuit. He was also interested in writing and devoting time to that. I was ready to make time for me and my interests outside of the shop. I wanted time to relax, meditate, and explore other interests such as metaphysics.

We gave my sisters notice that in six months we would be leaving the shop. We needed the six months to wind down and wrap things up. This time was important because I needed to align with the decision. Leaving was not easy. It was our main source of income, and money (or lack of) was an issue for me. The idea of losing that security was a major fear I had to deal with. Though I felt drawn to do something different with my life, I had no idea what that would be.

I'd been working hard to overcome my trust and fear issues, but it was not an easy task. If I wanted to change my life, I needed to let go of the fears and doubts about the future and trust everything would work out fine. Something that was a great help were these past life memories that came to me spontaneously on three separate occasions:

NATIVE AMERICAN MAN

I was considering getting back into hypnotherapy and wanted to work on a script to use with future clients. I wasn't trying to do a past life regression, but I guess the script I was coming up with was a pretty good one because suddenly there I was in another time and place. At first, I watched from the shadows. People were hurrying about the streets and wagons were being driven up and down the road. The women wore long dresses and bonnets on their heads. The men dressed in drab pants and baggy coats.

There was a row of wooden structures facing one another on either side of the muddy dirt road.

Looking past the end of the settlement and high up on a hill I saw myself, a Native American with a large headdress and a spear, sitting on my horse and observing the scene below. As I now viewed the scene from the hill top, I watched the people scurrying to and fro in such a hurry. I did not understand these strangers, these soulless people who had no connection to the earth or to the sky. No connection to the Gods. I took no action, I just observed.

A couple months later this past life came to me:

NATIVE AMERICAN WOMAN

I gazed at my reflection in the cool clear water. Looking back at me was a young woman with a pleasing face and soft smiling eyes. Her dark hair was in braids with a single feather hanging down. As I knelt by the water I was at peace. Life was good.

I stood, let my heavy dress drop to the ground, and stepped into the water. Enjoying this quiet time to myself, I gave thanks for the beauty around me. This was a favorite spot with the rock walls and gushing waterfall at one end of the pool that narrowed to a gentle stream flanked by open meadows at the opposite end. The pool was hugged on either side by tall pines, allowing a feeling of being completely alone with nature and my thoughts. This was a time to relax and appreciate all of the blessings in my life.

After taking my time swimming and floating in the refreshing water, gazing into the blue sky and feeling the warmth of the sun on my face, I knew it was time to go. I'd indulged myself long enough. As I stood and walked toward the river bank, I was startled by the sight of a man on horseback, intently watching me from the river's edge. I smiled. It was my husband. We hadn't been married long and we were very much in love.

We took this rare opportunity to be alone and made love in the meadow. When we finished, I slipped into my dress and my husband took my hand, pulling me up and onto the back of his horse. I wrapped my arms around him and nestled my face into his shoulder, feeling his strong muscles and taking in the earthy scent of his sweaty body. I was happy. Love felt so good.

That was when the shot rang out. We both were thrown from his horse to the ground below. My husband was dead. I was soon captured. The white men took me away. I don't remember much about what happened next, but that evening, although I was bound and blindfolded, I could tell there was a campfire with several men sitting around it, laughing, drinking, and bragging about what they'd done that day—killing the savage and taking me as a prize.

Eventually I made it back to my people, but I was never the same. None of us were. Life had changed. We used to be a happy people. We lived in peace and believed in ourselves and our ways. Our people respected life, the land, and the animals. We gave thanks to our Gods and trusted we would be taken care of. Now we lived in fear. Fear of the white men and their brutal ways. We'd lost our connection to ourselves, our faith, our trust. We let fear take over our lives.

Many years had passed as I stared at the dark sky filled with so many stars and asked, "How did we let this happen?"

Another couple of months later this memory came to me.

I looked down at my feet as I often do when going into a past life. I saw snow shoes and the ground below them that was covered with the purest white snow I'd ever seen. Moving my focus back to get a better look at myself, I saw that I was heavily bundled in furs and animal skins. My hood covered most of my face and at first I thought I was a man. As the image became clearer I realized it was not a male figure I was seeing, but a young female. One that I'd seen before. The same Native American woman I first saw a couple of months ago.

Looking at the scenery around me, it was absolutely incredible. I was on a snow-covered ridge that seemed to be entirely untouched by man. The snow was pure white with not even an animal track to disturb its smooth, crispy surface. To my left were enormously tall trees with the sun shining through them and brilliantly reflecting on the snow. The sky was a bright blue and the air was cold, crisp, and clean. I stood there marveling at the beauty and gazing at the valley below. I was close to home. I could feel it. Somehow, I had found my way.

I pulled the animal skins away from my chest just far enough to peek down and check on the baby who was peacefully sleeping in their warmth. I looked with love at the last gift my husband had given me.

Forced into servitude by one of the white men who captured me, I cooked and cleaned for his family. I gained their trust by taking care of the household chores and doing what was asked of me. But my child needed to know his people, and he was not going to grow up to be a slave. When the time was right, I took the items I needed to survive and we quietly left during the night. I did not like taking what did not belong to me, but I needed the snowshoes and furs to survive. And it was, after all, far less than what they'd taken from me.

I have dealt with trust issues all my life for apparent reasons. At the time these memories came out I'd been working hard on finding a way to trust—both myself and the universe. I'd been trying to let go of fear and not let it hold me back, to trust that all was well and everything would work out for me. It has been my experience that past life memories come to me when there is a connection between events lived through in a previous life and what I am currently going through. In that life, at some level, I lost my trust in God (or the universe). Fear crippled not only me but my people as a whole. It was our downfall.

There have been so many times since these memories came to me that I have gone back and reread the story of what happened and regained the courage to move forward. Because of these memories I found the strength and determination in this life to not let fear defeat me again. I often think about that past life and how not only I, but all of my people in that life, let fear separate us from who we truly were.

CHAPTER 28

Letting Go

BY DECEMBER 31ST, THE END OF our six months' notice, I'd found my alignment and was ready to let go of the security of the shop and open myself up for a new adventure. I felt at peace with my decision and excited about what was to come. Still not having any clue as to what I would be doing in the future, I was not sure how to proceed. I knew I needed to meditate, journal, and channel on a more regular basis, but beyond that I needed answers.

For several years I'd thought about putting my life experiences on paper. I had my journals, but I wanted to document specific incidents more thoroughly. The thought played in my head, but I never got around to actually doing anything about it. I questioned the benefit of it. Would it just be dredging up the past or would it add to my healing? The urge was getting stronger, so I began to put my most significant experiences down on paper. It just seemed to be something I needed to do for my own healing. My writing would just be for my eyes. Maybe someday, after I was gone, my children would read my words and better understand me.

Still trying to figure out what my next step in life would be, I decided to attend a New Year's Day psychic fair that was being held to raise funds for animal rescue. It was for a good cause, it could be fun, and maybe I could get some insight into the path that lay ahead of me. As soon as I sat down with the psychic medium, the information started pouring out. What stood out to me the most was that she saw me penning a book and that it would come together through writing that I had already done. This seemed strange to me because aside from my journaling, I was not a writer at all. But the thought of writing a book stayed on my mind. As I considered all the journaling and channeling I had done over the years, as well as the recent accounts I had begun to write, I could see a book coming together. What cemented the idea was a title that popped into my mind—*Frozen Children*.

So now with more free time on my hands and a nudge from the psychic (and the universe), I began to seriously work on my memoirs. By mid-January when Glenn and I left for a vacation in Sedona, Arizona, I had chronicled many incidents from my childhood and years of remembering and healing. I'd been telling Glenn for some time that I wanted him to read some of my writings, whenever he was ready. He knew the basics of what I went through as a child and had some idea of my healing process, but it was often difficult to express myself clearly when we talked, and I never felt like he actually understood the impact any of it had on me. We agreed that while on vacation he would read the excerpts from my life that I'd written so far.

Once in Sedona, I sat in the bedroom while he read in another room. When he finished, he came in, put his arms around me, and apologized for not having been there for me in a stronger way. We talked a lot and I felt closer to him than ever. For the first time I felt like I could tell him anything and everything. We shared our hopes and dreams for the future. We both were anxious to pursue interests that we'd had no time for while working in our retail business. Glenn was taking writing classes and I wanted to continue getting my memories down on paper. I was interested in spending more time studying metaphysics and Glenn also hoped to spend time advancing his knowledge in other areas. We hoped the new pursuits would eventually open doors for us to be of service to others. Glenn and I were eager to support one another.

We visited several metaphysical shops while in Sedona. We'd talked about getting a "couples" reading as well as individual readings during our trip. After looking around one shop for a while, Glenn was ready to leave. He wasn't prepared to get his individual reading yet, but I was feeling a strong urge to get our couples reading and a woman named Joyea was available. I'd begun studying the Archangels on the advice I received from my reading earlier in the month. Although I'd called upon Archangel Michael and asked for his assistance many times over the years, I didn't know much about most of the archangels. As Joyea started the reading she announced that four powerful archangels had immediately joined us. The messages we got were encouraging. They confirmed where we were headed and that things would go well for us. Several times during the reading Glenn and I looked at each other and laughed. Joyea was so accurate and touched on the subjects we'd been discussing earlier in the day, such as our writing, the need for an editor, our desire to grow spiritually, and our new direction in life. This was a powerful message. I needed to continue writing, trusting the universe, and trusting myself. It was no longer a matter of if things would happen, it was a matter of when.

It had taken a lot for me to align my energy enough to feel good about leaving the financial security of my job, but it just didn't feel like

I was supposed to be there anymore. When I finally let go of the worry and decided to trust that the universe would take care of me, I had no idea what path I would be taking. I'd been trying to control the course of my life and point it in the direction I thought it should take. When it didn't seem to be going there, I gave up and asked the universe to show me the way. Within a few days, I was given the idea to write the book. It wasn't long before I received a notice that large dividends from some stock I owned would be distributed throughout the year. I was grateful for the unexpected money flowing to me, assuring me of the income I needed to get through the year. I had finally put my trust in the universe and the universe did not disappoint me.

I'm not sure if anyone ever completely heals from the abuse suffered in childhood, or any major trauma for that matter, but I feel good about where I am today—trusting the universe, believing life is good, expecting good things to happen. Oh, and that imaginary graph line that shows my moods . . . the line often goes way above the even point now. When I first began experiencing joy for no good reason, Glenn would look at me and want to know what was up. "What was I hiding?" he asked. I wasn't hiding anything. I was just happy.

About the Author

In her late thirties, Shelley Johnson's life forever changed when repressed childhood memories began to surface. She has spent years dealing with the aftermath of these memories. In her book, Frozen Children, she takes you on her journey through her darkest days and into the light where she now lives.

Her journey has been guided by her interest in metaphysics and spirituality. Along the way she has obtained certification as a Clinical Hypnotherapist and a Reiki Master. Shelley has used these techniques, as well as other alternative methods, throughout her healing process.

Born in upstate New York, she now resides in the Atlanta area with her husband. They have recently retired from the antiques and resale business and enjoy traveling, especially when visiting their children and granddaughter.

Acknowledgments

My deepest love and gratitude to my husband Glenn for his unfaltering support and encouragement throughout the entire process of writing this book. Without his help, editorial comments, and reassurance, it may never have left my computer.

To Henry Carrigan and Jennifer Avery for their editing suggestions on my early drafts.

To Belinda, Sara, Carolyn, and Johanna for their prepublication reviews and comments.

To Vikki, Denise, Richard, Suzie, and Diane for their support, feedback, and encouragement after reading advanced reader copies.

Thank you to Nanette Littlestone for editing this book and pushing me to dig deeper.

Also, thanks to all my metaphysical friends, energy workers, and counselors who guided me through my early days of healing.

Lastly, thanks to my Divine Board of Directors and my non-physical supporters.

Excerpts from this book:

"Shock, denial, disbelief, rationalization, and finally acceptance, then more denial, doubt, and not wanting to believe. These were just a few of the stages I went through [...]."

"We each have our own way of dealing with abuse and painful issues. For some, the abuse or pain strengthens them and pushes them to overcome [...]. Others, like me, internalize it, hide it, and hope to keep it safely stowed away in some deep, dark part of ourselves."

"I had one especially bad episode of depression that ended in a way I'll never forget. I was in an awful state. The hopelessness I felt was deeper than any I'd ever experienced up until that point. There was no way out. I'd had enough."

"When I'm down on myself, I often must remind myself of how the universe feels about me, about every one of us. We are loved unconditionally. Always. No matter what."

"I'd been trying to control the course of my life and point it in the direction I thought it should take. When it didn't seem to be going there, I gave up and asked the universe to show me the way. Within a few days..."

www.ingramcontent.com/pod-product-compliance
Lightning Source LLC
Chambersburg PA
CBHW032032050726
47590CB00006B/2389